Ralph Waldo Emerson

Twayne's United States Authors Series

Lewis Leary, Editor
University of North Carolina, Chapel Hill

TUSAS 414

RALPH WALDO EMERSON
(1803–1882)

Ralph Waldo Emerson

By Donald Yannella

University of Southern Mississippi

Twayne Publishers • Boston

Ralph Waldo Emerson

Donald Yannella

Copyright © 1982 by G. K. Hall & Company
Published by Twayne Publishers
A Division of G. K. Hall & Company
70 Lincoln Street
Boston, Massachusetts 02111

Book Production by Marne B. Sultz

Book Design by Barbara Anderson

Printed on permanent/durable acid-free
paper and bound in the United States of
America.

**Library of Congress Cataloging in
Publication Data**

Yannella, Donald.
Ralph Waldo Emerson.

(Twayne's United States authors series ;
TUSAS 414)
Bibliography: p. 139
Includes index.
    1. Emerson, Ralph Waldo, 1803–
1882—Criticism   and   interpretation.
I. Title II. Series.
PS1638.Y36   814'.3   81-20321
ISBN 0-8057-7344-4   AACR2

To our memories of my Father
and Mother, Donald and Johanna,
and to my children—Susan,
Katherine, Donald, Christopher,
and Clare—who have
"Prospects"

Contents

About the Author

Donald Yannella, who received the Ph.D. from Fordham University, is professor and chairman of the department of English at the University of Southern Mississippi; from 1964 to 1981 he taught at Glassboro State College. In addition to articles and reviews published in a number of journals, he was coauthor of *American Prose to 1820* (1979) and is presently completing an edition of the Diaries of Evert A. Duyckinck. He has been an officer in The Melville Society since 1972 and for the past seven years has edited the quarterly *Melville Society Extracts*. Mr. Yannella is also serving as secretary-treasurer of the American Literature Section of the Modern Language Association.

Preface

Perhaps I should say here at the beginning that I have written this introduction to Ralph Waldo Emerson not for specialists in the literature of nineteenth-century America but for general readers. Of course, such a group is large and even amorphous, so for a working guide I have kept in mind the segment of it which I know best: college students of whatever age, people who are interested in American literature or, for that matter, any other aspect of our cultural history. My long experience instructing these representatives of the general audience has taught me that they are generally intelligent, enthusiastic, inquisitive, and eager to work hard if the subject to be explored is interesting and useful. Emerson is both. To touch such an audience the trick, of course, is not to presume that they know too much and are more sophisticated than they actually are. I hope I have not. On the other hand, one cannot be so elementary as to be patronizing. I trust I have avoided this pitfall, too. These problems one encounters when writing for a general audience are compounded by my subject himself. For no matter how one tries to reduce and simplify and clarify, the fact remains that Emerson is a difficult writer. He is not impossible, however, and his thought and writing are so enormously important and inherently interesting that few readers in the end feel that their rewards do not match the energy and time they have expended.

This book concentrates on the essays and poems—he wrote no fiction or plays—he published in his lifetime because these are unquestionably the place to begin one's study. One should probably save the almost twenty-five hefty volumes of his journals, lectures, and letters for later, although they are, in fact, essential if one is to pursue Emerson seriously. My arrangement is essentially chronological: Chapter 1 offers a brief biographical sketch and places Emerson among the events he lived through. Chapter 2 and the larger part of Chapter 3 concentrate on his early, radical period; I dwell on this for it is of such crucial importance to his career and to our understanding of him. There is a short description of Transcendentalism in the first chapter, but I would suggest that the reader be patient and not expect even a marginally firm grasp of the movement and his place in it until after reading the second and third chapters, at least. The latter part of Chapter 3 and most of Chapter 5 focus principally on his middle period, and his less important late period is given brief treatment at the end of Chapter 5. Chapter 4 centers on his poetry, which it seems is more readily introduced by being discussed separately. Chapter 6, my conclusion, reviews Emerson's reputation, influence, and place in our cultural history, suggests some of the reasons he is important, and directs the reader to a few avenues that might be traveled in pursuing this rich and elusive author. The chapter titles, excepting the last, are Emerson's own words, and the sources of all but the first, which is from "History," are to be found in the chapters they head.

You might read the essays and poems as you work through this study or after completing it. In the hope that you will continue your work in Emerson, you will find suggested readings in the Selected Bibliography at the end of the book. You might also broaden your understanding by reading some of the sources in the Notes and References which offer more detailed discussions of subjects I only touch.

Perhaps the ten feet of bookshelf space occupied by Emerson's writings and those of his critics speak more forcefully for his importance than I can. In any case, the volumes and articles are at once intimidating and enormously helpful. My obligation to those scholars I have followed is great, and I trust that my notes acknowledge most if not all my debts; if I have omitted references to anyone's work I seem to have benefited from, it is only because I have absorbed the source too well—a compliment, perhaps.

Finally, I wish to thank Lewis Leary, my editor, whose useful suggestions, graciously offered, have improved the book; and Kathleen, my wife, whose patience and practical help in proofreading have been, as usual, important.

Donald Yannella

University of Southern Mississippi

Chronology

1840   *The Dial* commences publication.

1841   *Essays: First Series* is published; daughter Edith is born.

1842   Son Waldo dies; begins to edit *The Dial*.

1844   *The Dial* ceases publication; son Edward Waldo is born; *Essays: Second Series* is published.

1846   *Poems* is published.

1847–1848   Goes to Europe; visits England and France.

1849   *Nature, Addresses, and Lectures,* a retrospective collection, is published.

1850   *Representative Men* is published.

1851   Lectures against the Fugitive Slave Act and commences activism in the abolitionist cause.

1856   *English Traits* is published.

1860   *The Conduct of Life* is published.

1866   *May-Day and Other Pieces* is published.

1870   *Society and Solitude* is published.

1871   Journeys to California.

1872–1873   Goes to Europe; visits France, Italy, Egypt, Greece, and British Isles.

1875   *Letters and Social Aims* is published.

1876   *Selected Poems* is published.

1882   April 27, Emerson dies.

Chapter One
A Rare, Extravagant Spirit

When Ralph Waldo Emerson was born in the spring of 1803, no one, of course, could have imagined the greening he would bring to American life. The young nation, having itself been delivered after no small labor scarcely fifteen years earlier, offered fertile ground for cultivation and would in turn nourish the tillers of our intellectual and literary landscape. Few Americans would bring forth shoots as sturdy as Emerson's. His, however, were to be hybrids of a more robust and life-sustaining variety than promised by his roots, which were sunk deep into the institutions and history of his native New England.

Emerson's paternal forebears had occupied the pulpit of the Congregational Church in Concord, Massachusetts, for all but thirty-two years since 1635, and these several decades included the ministry of his step-grandfather.[1] Although a few of these men had been touched by the religious renewal of the Great Awakening in the mid-eighteenth century, they had for the most part been orthodox clergymen, playing significant if minor roles in colonial history. The infant boy's paternal grandfather, who was to die of a fever while serving as chaplain to the Revolutionary forces, had been engaged in the politics of the volatile period, even recruiting Minutemen; and the famous battle against the British at the old North Bridge had been fought close by the Old Manse these ministers of the Concord Congregational Church inhabited.

His father, William, was a man of modest intellectual bent who possessed tastes for the arts, music, and literature. After his marriage in 1796 to Ruth Haskins, the tenth of distiller John Haskins's sixteen children, William supplemented his meager revenues as a clergyman by keeping a school in Harvard, Massachusetts, the town thirty miles from Boston in which the young couple settled. A Unitarian, his dissatisfactions were fed by his poverty. As the new century was about to be born, his hopes for a more liberal congregation were fulfilled when Boston's First Church, the Old Brick, called him. Although financial

1

problems continued to nag the growing household, William's new parish offered infinitely more cultural stimulation and opportunity than the young minister had experienced in the provincial environs of his earlier ministry. A few months following the birth of Ralph Waldo, their fourth child and third son (they were to have six boys and two girls), William even had the pleasure of seeing some of his sermons in print. Never a Unitarian radical, he was a genteel and mannered man who was drawn to the security of established prosperity and, in keeping with his conservative Federalist politics, distrusted the threat of excessive democratization. Shortly after the founding of the *Monthly Anthology,* the predecessor of the prestigious and long-lived *North American Review,* William became its editor; but within a few years, in 1808, he showed the first symptoms of the consumption that was to claim him in 1811, a few weeks before young Ralph's eighth birthday. As a minister, public servant, and author, William Emerson's achievements were conventional and modest. His widow, Ruth, left to struggle constantly against poverty while raising her large family, was a plain and pious woman who managed the family's affairs with good sense and integrity.

Ralph, who appeared perfectly average, had started school early— evidently before he was three years of age—and commenced his studies at the rigorous Boston Latin School in 1812; in the same year, as the young nation's second war with England broke out, the boy made his first attempts at writing poetry. Leaving the chaos of the war-threatened harbor town in which she had been running boarding houses, Ruth Emerson took the family to Concord in 1814, where they remained until the spring of 1815. While residing in the Old Manse with his grandmother Emerson and his step-grandfather Ripley, young Ralph pursued his verse-making and attended school.

Back in Boston, while Ruth struggled to make ends meet, principally by catering to boarders in a succession of establishments, Ralph continued his studies and, following several generations of his ancestors, entered Harvard College in 1817. Having been well-grounded at the Latin School in the classical languages, for example, Emerson was adequately prepared for his collegiate studies, even though he was somewhat younger than the average young man in the class of '21. Drawn to history and public speaking—one of the period's enthusiasms—he continued to write and even became class poet, though he evidently was not the first choice for the honor. Harvard's curriculum was traditional and structured, and he seems to have enjoyed college life. Throughout his career in Cambridge he received financial help and aided in meeting expenses by teaching during vacation periods. His studies in areas such as literature and philosophy—he was always weak in mathematics—were enhanced by some eminent Harvard faculty, including Edward Everett, George Ticknor, Edward Tyrrel Channing, and the older Levi Frisbie. But his serious work in subjects such as the German thinkers and Scottish philosophers, especially Reid and Stewart, was nicely balanced by social club activities, particularly those concerned with religious issues, great books, and also composition and oratory. His "Dissertation on the Present State of Ethical Philosophy" won one of two seconds. Emerson's college years were a mixture of healthy social activity and intellectual development. On the summer day in 1821 when he graduated, he ranked thirtieth in a class of fifty-nine young American scholars.

By the end of the year, Waldo—the middle name he had indicated a preference for by the end of his college days—was teaching in his older brother William's school for young women. For the next several years, while carrying out these responsibilities, he used what spare time he could find to read and even write, not only his poetry but also some fiction, drama criticism, and essays. The ambitious young man's sense of getting nowhere significant in life was hardly offset by his first publication, an essay in the *Christian Disciple,* late in 1822: "Thoughts on the Religion of the Middle Ages," which appeared anonymously. With his brother William off to Germany in 1823 to study for the ministry, Waldo and his younger brother Edward continued to run schools, but Waldo thirsted to begin his own religious studies. Channing, his former teacher, encouraged him, even while William's letters chronicled growing doubts about his own vocation; but at the end of 1824 Ralph Waldo finally closed his school for young women and entered the middle class of the Harvard Divinity School the following February. Within a month, however, he was having difficulty with his eyes which finally led him to leave his studies and open a country school. During the next few years he was plagued by health problems, including rheumatism and difficulty in the lungs, as he tried to maintain a succession of schools. It seems probable that his genuine physical ailments were aggravated by the psychological difficulties he was suffering as he began studies to become a clergyman. And so, following medical advice, he set sail late in November 1826 for Charleston, South Carolina, and proceeded to St. Augustine early in the new year, where he stayed for some two-and-one-half months. While in Florida he enjoyed the challenging, even disturbing company of the atheist Achille Murat, the nephew of Napoleon. On his way back to New England he stopped in New York to visit his brother William, who, having dropped plans for the ministry, was studying law, the profession he was to follow in that city until his death in 1868. Recovered from his ailments after a few years away from his formal studies, Emerson took his room in Divinity Hall at Harvard in 1827.

Having received his license to preach the year before, his reputation as a skillful pulpit orator was building. It was while preaching in Concord, New Hampshire, on Christmas Day 1827, that the twenty-four-year-old man met Ellen Tucker, who was seven years younger. Following a courtship which intensified over more than a year and a half, they were married late in September 1829. Earlier in the year Emerson had been called as junior pastor to Boston's Second Church, formerly the church of Increase and Cotton Mather, and been ordained into the ministry. By the time they were married he was well settled into the routines of parish work, conducting services and supporting those who needed him. But almost from the beginning of the marriage his young bride declined from the tuberculosis she had been living with. She died early in 1831, scarcely a year and a half after their wedding.

The widower continued to pursue his pastoral work and even labored hard for the School Committee, to which he had been elected. But during 1831 his interest began to center on literature—especially the writings of contemporaries such as Carlyle, Coleridge, Wordsworth, and Goethe—as his enthusiasm for the church waned. Toward the end of 1832 he had his final falling out with his congregation and, finally, to the dismay of most of his family, resigned his ministry. The two years past had been psychologically and spiritually trying and his health had again begun to slip. On Christmas Day 1832 he sailed for Europe, where the cares and trials of the recent past would recede, even if he could not abolish them. His health improved as he journeyed through Italy, and on to Geneva, Paris, and London. After bathing in the classical world he discovered in Sicily, he was drawn to the usual tourist attractions of Rome—even witnessing Easter mass celebrated by the

Pope in St. Peter's—and was enchanted by the art and music of Florence, where he began his rich relationship with the American sculptor Horatio Greenough. Paris, a politically vibrant city, was another adventure in the fine and performing arts and also offered the riches of its museums of natural history and science. By July 1833, when he crossed the Channel to London, the distresses which had sent him abroad seemed distant.

The British Isles, in their way, proved to be even more important to the young ex-minister than the Continent had been. He visited John Stuart Mill, among many other notables, but was most touched by his journeys to see Coleridge, Wordsworth, and especially Carlyle, with whom he commenced a lifelong friendship. Refreshed and vital, he left Liverpool in September and the following month arrived in New York, then returned to Boston.

Shortly after coming back to America, Emerson commenced his career as a lecturer, which was to provide the principal source of his income for the rest of his life. His anxiety about money was alleviated immediately when he inherited some $11,000, half of Ellen's share of the Tucker legacy, which provided him an all-important financial cushion.[2] But these advances in fortune were darkened by the death of his brother Edward late in 1834, another victim of the period's scourge, tuberculosis.

Somewhat more than a year after his return, Emerson became engaged to Lydia Jackson of Plymouth, Massachusetts. Eight years his senior, Lydia—or, as he preferred, Lidian—was a highly intelligent, well-informed woman whose roots, like his own, reached into early colonial New England. Although she had been raised in a rather strict Calvinist atmosphere, at the time of their marriage in September 1835 she was a religious seeker, who went so far as to flirt with Swedenborgian mysticism, even though she was nominally a Unitarian. At the time of their wedding, her flexibility, her willingness to explore the intellectual and spiritual landscape, made her well suited to share his life. As the years passed, however, and Emerson remained uncompromising in his philosophical radicalism, Lidian was to become more conservative. Their marriage was stable but staid; for Emerson the passions ignited by his first wife seem to have remained banked.

The dozen years following Emerson's second marriage and his first book, *Nature,* a year later in 1836, form the most creative period of his thinking, writing, and speaking. He was at the peak of his energies and took his place as the principal spokesman for the New England Transcendental movement. The late 1830s and early 1840s mark the high point of his publicly spoken Idealism as well as the beginning and firming of his fruitful relationships with Henry Thoreau, Bronson Alcott, Margaret Fuller, and other Transcendentalists. Almost five years elapsed between the appearance of his first volume and his second, *Essays: First Series,* in March 1841, but he was not idle. In addition to establishing himself more firmly as a popular and financially successful lecturer, he delivered two major addresses at Harvard—"The American Scholar" (1837) and the "Divinity School Address" (1838). He also labored hard on the Transcendental quarterly, *The Dial,* which he helped found in 1840, and in 1844 he published *Essays: Second Series.* This was to be followed in late 1846 by *Poems,* his first collection of the verses he had been composing for more than twenty years.

In 1838 the break he had begun early in the decade with the Unitarian church, and for that matter organized Christianity, widened and was finally completed with the address he delivered before the Divinity School. His collision with the institution to which his ties were strongest—his falling away had probably begun in the early 1820s[3]—was the result of a painful necessity and was effected by remarkable honesty and courage. Emerson's sensitivity had been well demonstrated a decade earlier by the close inspection to which he had subjected himself when he was on the threshold of his ministry. His doubts were probably as much a matter of temperament as of intellectual conviction. And the questions, the indecisions, had continued as he went through the crisis which culminated in his resigning his pulpit in 1832. The path Emerson had been following and cutting for some fifteen years before his Sunday evening in 1838 at the Divinity School had been difficult, but he had continued on it.

These years were also fraught with deep personal pain. This man who had lost his father a few weeks before his eighth birthday and borne the death in 1831 of his bride, Ellen, also suffered those of his brothers Edward and Charles, in 1834 and 1836; and he was then to lose his beloved five-year-old son, Waldo, in 1842. He developed and embraced his Transcendental philosophy in the face of adversity.

Seeing him within the contexts of his personal problems and religious crises is essential, but it is also important to recognize that

Emerson was profoundly influenced by the events taking place in nineteenth-century America. The new nation was not yet fifteen years of age, its Declaration of Independence from Great Britain scarcely more than a quarter-century in the past, when Emerson was born in the small walking city of Boston. During the almost eighty years of his life he witnessed dramatic changes in his culture. For example, during the first fifty years of the nineteenth century, Emerson and his contemporaries saw the births of the steamboat, the railroad, the telegraph, and the daguerreotype, to mention only a few of the more dramatic inventions which altered life. At the same time that the first mass-production systems were developing in Emerson's native New England, the nation paused on the threshold of its geographical expansion westward, a movement which remains unmatched in its speed and thoroughness in the history of Man. These changes in which American culture was caught up were parallel to developments in European culture of the period. The winds of change whipped through the worlds of science, politics, and virtually every other aspect of Western life, including literature and philosophy. The period was informed by hopes and by visions.

Emerson's early writings continue to beat with the rhythms and fevers of the second quarter of the century. Although never a champion of Andrew Jackson, who represented a coarseness and vulgarity he could not abide, Emerson nevertheless supported the democratization and expansion which were in process. At least if their purposes were rightly understood and his distinctions and discriminations accepted. Certainly, his individualism, his belief in democracy, his support of the ordinary, and his optimism were in keeping with the Frontier spirit which informed the Jacksonian period. But Emerson was not a staunch supporter of Manifest Destiny. Always suspicious of popular mass movements and easy definitions of purpose and belief, he was more skeptical and conservative about "Progress" than most of his contemporaries.[4] What he feared—and as events unfolded his fears were substantiated—was that the westward expansion and new industrialism would find their fulfillment in a gross materialism, a prosperity born of exploitation.[5]

For the most part detached from the everyday workings of the period, Emerson was and remains one of the most sensitive observers of the broader, more important currents of his time—its aspirations and fears, its consciousness of being engaged in dramatic change. Never a "booster," an "upstart,"[6] Emerson nevertheless breathed the period's spirit time and again in his private and public utterances. Swept up in the material wealth afforded by a fast-moving and fluid society, America was in a boom period. Emerson watched and understood the forces at work. But he steadfastly refused to give himself to them, as he told his audience most pointedly at the conclusion of his fourth lecture on "The Times" in 1841. He asked them whether, "Amidst the downward tendency and proneness" toward materialism, they would "tolerate one or two solitary voices in the land, speaking for thoughts and principles not marketable or perishable?" (*CW*, I, 216).

The rapidity and seriousness of the culture's transitions are perhaps most evident in the social and political changes of this volatile period. Jacksonian America saw the vested interests of the old Federalists and business-oriented Whigs challenged by the raw, husky assertions of common men. Sectional and socioeconomic interests collided with stunning reverberations. As monied interests were challenged—for example, in Jackson's battle with Nicholas Biddle's Bank—the laboring classes made their initial moves toward unionization, and more and more of them secured the franchise. The industrial revolution with its technology gained momentum as the frontier loomed larger and more attractive and cities began to grow by leaps and bounds. Change and growth were the keynotes as old alliances dissolved and new ones formed.

Emerson's sensitivity to these changes is probably nowhere better illustrated than in his eight lectures on "The Times," delivered in the 1841–42 season. In the first he offers a succinct catalogue of some of the most important issues to which America had been addressing itself for more than a decade: "the Banks; the Tariff; the limits of the executive power; the right of the constituent to instruct the representative; the treatment of the Indians; the Boundary wars; the Congress of nations." To Emerson all these are "pregnant with ethical conclusions" (*CW*, I, 173). And he leaves no doubt about whose side he was on; rejecting the conservatives, he characterizes the reformers, these innovators, these "leaders of the crusades against War, Negro slavery, Intemperance, Government based on force . . . and so on to the agitators on the system of Education and the laws of Property," as "the right successors of Luther, Knox, Robinson, Fox, Penn, Wesley, and Whitfield" (*CW*,

I, 172). Yet he has reservations about these movers and shakers; they "affirm the inward life, but they do not trust it, but use outward and vulgar means. They do not rely on precisely that strength which wins me to their cause; not on love, not on a principle, but on men, on multitudes, on circumstances, on money, on party; that is, on fear, on wrath, and pride" (*CW*, I, 176).

It is in the fourth lecture, "The Transcendentalist," that Emerson presents his real hero in conflict with the Materialist who "insists on facts, on history, on the force of circumstances, and the animal wants of man." Transcendentalism is "Idealism as it appears in 1842"; its adherents "perceive that the senses are not final, and say, the senses give us representations of things, but what are the things themselves, they cannot tell" (*CW*, I, 201). He admits that these Transcendentalists "are not good citizens, not good members of society . . . . do not even like to vote" (*CW*, I, 210–11). In the "Introductory Lecture" he had warned that "Their unbelief arises out of a greater Belief; their inaction out of a scorn of inadequate action. By the side of these men, the hot agitators have a certain cheap and ridiculous air" (*CW*, I, 180). He prefers spectators to actors and concludes "The Transcendentalist" with a plea, couched in ironic understatement, for society to be charitable toward them: "In our Mechanics' Fair, there must be not only bridges, ploughs, carpenters' planes, and baking troughs, but also some few finer instruments . . . and in society, besides farmers, sailors, and weavers, there must be a few persons of purer fire kept specially as gauges and meters of character; persons of a fine, detecting instinct, who note the smallest accumulations of wit and feeling in the bystander." Arriving circuitously at his point, he adds, "Perhaps too there might be room for the exciters and monitors; collectors of the heavenly spark with power to convey the electricity to others" (*CW*, I, 216). Such a person Emerson strived to be.

No mere ivory-tower intellectual, he was a thinker and poet profoundly in touch with his contemporaries and the culture he shared with them. That he chose to step back from the fray and, as he describes the posture in "The American Scholar," "not quit his belief that a popgun is a popgun, though the ancient and honorable of the earth affirm it to be the crack of doom" (*CW*, I, 63), remains our good fortune. Perhaps he achieved the distance from his period—and as a result saw it more clearly than most of his contemporaries—because he recognized that "what are called *new views* here in New England . . . are not new, but the very oldest of thoughts cast into the mould of these new times" (*CW*, I, 201). More important, though, he observed the period as a Transcendentalist.

To understand Emerson's observations, analyses, and responses to his times it is crucial to comprehend the Transcendental movement and its background in Unitarianism. Dissent, even in the form of religious enthusiasm, had a modest history in the Emerson family. Waldo's great-grandfather had labored with George Whitefield during the Great Awakening, the revival movement which swept the colony in the 1740s, and his father played a small role in Unitarianism's challenge to New England orthodoxy. The Unitarian movement which began in the Boston area during the late eighteenth century was, in the period's terminology, another blossoming of Arminianism, a rebirth of the heresy that Man could in fact substantially contribute to his own salvation. Seriously intellectual, Unitarians challenged the emotionalism of the Second Great Awakening which swept the country in the 1790s and insisted on religious freedom and congregational autonomy. Less an original position than a new synthesis, Unitarianism reflected and articulated the optimism of the Enlightenment and the aspirations of the new nation;[7] the people it attracted were for the most part cultured and intellectual, among the elite of American society.

In the process of supplanting their predecessors, who were moderate Calvinists, the Unitarians enjoyed their most significant political gains at Harvard in 1805 and 1806 when Henry Ware was elected Hollis Professor of Divinity and Samuel Webber was chosen president.[8] But even by the 1830s, when the Unitarians themselves were challenged by Emerson and his fellow Transcendentalists, Unitarianism remained fluid, less a formal movement or sect than a liberal persuasion.[9] Given this older generation's liberal spirit of generosity and their hard-won successes in the more than thirty year battle with the conservative Calvinist establishment, it is little wonder that these liberals were outraged by the challenge with which Emerson and his fellow Transcendentalists presented them in the 1830s.

The Idealism Emerson and his fellow radicals asserted was in fact a hybrid and adapted Transcendentalism fed by many streams. While it was "essentially indigenous" to the New England world its professors inhabited,[10] it was nourished by Old World and even non-Western thought: Kantian and post-Kantian Idealism, as well as that of English contemporaries such as Coleridge and Carlyle; traditional Platonism and neo-Platonism, and modern Swedenborgianism; and Oriental systems, such as the Hindu, among other sources. The American group even formed the short-lived Transcendental Club which met for the first time on September 19, 1836, ten days after the publication of Emerson's first book, *Nature*. But the Transcendentalists never developed an effective organization. The fierce individualism at the heart of their belief actually precluded anything but a loose association. One of their major attempts at coming together, the Brook Farm utopian community organized mainly by George Ripley, disintegrated after only a few years, not only because of fiscal and organizational mismanagement but also due to the abiding independence of the farmers. Since one of the purposes of this study is a description of Emerson's Transcendentalism, we might consider briefly the movement's major repudiations and beliefs.

Reacting to what they considered the cold Lockean rationalism of Unitarianism, these young radicals relied heavily on spontaneous, intuitive insight as the principal and superior means Man might use in reaching toward the ultimates—truth, goodness, and beauty. Essentially Romantic from the point of view of the literary or cultural historian, the Transcendentalists' reliance on the emotions caused the greatest concern among the Unitarian fathers. The Transcendentalists insisted on genuine reliance on ideas, as opposed to the sensationalism of the Lockean system. While they rejected associationist psychology, which denied Man's conscious and active control of his mind, they asserted the higher imperatives of Reason (intuitive insight, Coleridge's Imagination) over the Understanding (the more pedestrian, logical, or rational faculties, Coleridge's Fancy). They viewed Nature, the Universe, as organic rather than mechanical; for the conception of a detached Deity in the systems of Newton and Paley, they substituted a corporeal, material Nature corresponding in all aspects to the world of Spirit, a universe suffused by the Deity. Among their other negations were the rituals of institutionalized religion, as well as Calvinistic notions of innate depravity and predestination; neoclassical formalism; and, finally, the more practical aspects of their Protestant heritage such as the work ethic and its corresponding insistence on the possibility of planned and controlled social order, a rational structuralism which guaranteed ultimate progress.

In place of the absolutes embraced by the older generation—and not all were affirmed by their own Unitarian fathers—the Transcendentalists asserted the divinity of Man and exhibited an abiding faith in the potential for his Genius to flourish were it to follow the lights of Reason. Practically, this led them to a vigorous individualism and a new focus on the rights and prerogatives of each person, even to the degree that these assertions by the individual might subvert the will of the majority which expressed itself by supporting civilized institutions.[11] The optimistic posture of these young Transcendentalists reflected the hopes which inspired the fledgling American nation in the liberal Jacksonian period, as well as the belief in progress associated with the Enlightenment and even some Romantic views. Irreverent about civilized institutions generally, the American Transcendentalists insisted upon the dignity, worth, authority, and responsibility of the single, separate person to a degree which would have been inconceivable to their Puritan ancestors and was utterly extreme from the point of view of their Unitarian fathers.[12]

Some nine months after the publication of his first collection of poems, America's most prominent Transcendentalist set sail for Europe for the second time. No longer the obscure and young former minister from New England, who had gone to Europe in the early 1830s to recover from the troubles which had befallen him and with the hope of meeting intellectual luminaries, Emerson was invited in 1847 to give a series of lectures in Old England. He had become something of a celebrity, and he approached the land of his ancestors with the perspective and confidence of an established intellectual. The engagements were to be highly successful and all in all the sojourn was as stimulating for him as his lectures were for his audiences.

He arrived in Liverpool in October 1847 and by visiting his old friend Carlyle in London commenced what would become a nine-month stay abroad. During the 1847–48 lecture season he offered courses in Liverpool and Manchester, where he resided, as well as a host of other towns in England and Scotland. Despite the organized opposition and protest with which conservatives, mostly churchmen, met him, the engagements were successful. When the season ended late in February he visited Wordsworth and then returned to London once again to visit Carlyle. London was caught up in the fever of the new French Revolution, and although Emerson observed the excitement of the Chartists in the capital, most of his time was taken up by aristocrats and intellectuals, including Dickens and Tennyson, who were anxious to entertain him. He attended the opera and theater, visited museums and other institutions, and even journeyed to the University at Oxford.

In May he was off to Paris where he settled in for a month on the Left Bank. Although the American celebrity stayed fairly close to the British colony in the French capital—he was not sufficiently fluent in the language to be comfortable with native Parisians—he enthusiastically pursued the usual cultural attractions and was swept up in the city's literary and theater life. But the most exciting events in progress were political; Emerson observed radicals such as Blanqui and even witnessed the storming of the National Assembly and similar displays of revolutionary fervor. He visited that perceptive observer of life in America, Alexis de Tocqueville, and left Paris with a more positive view of France and its citizens than he had brought.

Early in June he returned to London where he again lectured. A good deal of his time, however, was again taken up by the entertainments to which he was invited by aristocrats and intellectuals. Among the many authors with whom he spent time in the month before he boarded the ship home were Leigh Hunt, Thackeray, Douglas Jerrold, and, of course, the increasingly pessimistic Carlyle. The steamer made the crossing home in only twelve days—a far cry from the tedious, less comfortable passages of the sailing ships he had taken on his first trip abroad—and he arrived home in July 1848.

Lidian's health—she was in her fifties—was not good. But physically Emerson was flourishing to a degree he had rarely enjoyed before. Also evident was a certain mellowness; he was more relaxed and possessed an air of genial sociability, which was perhaps signaled best by his new pastime, cigar-smoking. The sight of the middle-age intellectual's head wreathed in smoke may have compromised preconceptions and earlier images of him—and might still—as austere, aloof, abstract—in a word, Transcendental. The mellowness was also reflected in his mounting passion for his gardening, especially the cultivation of his pear and other fruit trees, his enthusiastic participation in the social Town and Country Club, and the warm attention he paid to his children; it may also have been apparent in his cooler relations with Thoreau.

The events of the decade or so following his return to America after
this second trip are at once curious and understandable. The United
States was playing out the drama of upheaval which culminated in the
Civil War in 1861, and Emerson was gradually if inevitably drawn into
political debate and activity. Publicly, these years were neither quiet
nor settling. Shortly after returning from England he published the
first retrospective collection of his earlier prose writings, *Nature, Addresses, and Lectures* (1849). If he needed such support, the invitation to
gather his earlier prose certainly demonstrated the recognition he had
achieved in his brief thirteen-year career. At the same time, however,
the collection—a benchmark in any person's career—may have confirmed him in his nagging sense of age, his perception that his vigor
had diminished.[13]

The 1850s were not intellectually pioneering but they were product-
ive, if we are to use Emerson's publications as a measure. In 1850 there
was *Representative Men*—a subject he had been lecturing on for years and
had most recently used during his English tour—with its sketches of
Plato, the philosopher; Swedenborg, the mystic; Montaigne, the skeptic; Shakespeare, the poet; Napoleon, the man of the world; and
Goethe, the writer. *English Traits,* a volume that was written slowly and
with some difficulty and completed in a flurry of activity, was issued in
1856. In addition, Emerson continued on the lecture circuit, journey-
ing frequently as far west as Illinois and Wisconsin and traveling by
inland steamers, trains, and even stages. He sustained his popularity on
the circuit and was afforded the rare opportunity of viewing firsthand
the vital and fluid life of the young nation on the move.

Emerson's detachment from public affairs, his reluctance to engage
in active public life, was most severely tested and in the end compromised by the movement to abolish black slavery. During the debate
over the question, he entered the political arena which developed in the
1840s and 1850s; and in time Emerson identified and responded to the
moral question he came to see at the heart of the debate. His early
reluctance to participate actively in the movement for abolition was
caused by a variety of factors, not the least of which was his distrust of
philanthropy. From the 1830s he was suspicious of vocal abolitionists
such as Wendell Phillips, as well as of the crusade they led. Finding
their tactics distasteful, he held them off with the same reserve he
treated reformers and political factions in general; his posture was

founded on his temperament as well as on intellectual conviction. As the issue became more visible, however, and as personalities and bandwagons receded in his mind, he responded to it. The first major public evidence of his developing abolitionism was the speech he gave in Concord in 1844 on the tenth anniversary of West Indian Emancipation.[14] Here he revealed his diminished sympathy with slave-holding planters (his position had been that the problem was the South's) and exhibited an awakened tolerance of blacks; more important, he was now able to concentrate on the essential immorality and illegality of the "peculiar institution," despite the obfuscation created by the din of political exchange. Committed to emancipation by 1846 or 1847, at least privately, the public turning point came with Clay's Compromise of 1850, which was supported by his old hero, the senator from Massachusetts, Daniel Webster. The Fugitive Slave Law of that year outraged and further radicalized Emerson; he vented his fury by characterizing the law as a "filthy enactment" and swore that he would "not obey it, by God" (*JMN,* XI, 412); and his anger carried over into his public utterances.[15] While still somewhat willing to consider the issue as a local, moral problem with which the South must come to terms, he was adamant in his opposition to the extension of slavery into the territories of the West. John Brown's activities in Kansas, for example, enjoyed Emerson's support even before the two met in 1857; and Brown himself finally became a symbol of moral righteousness, even a type and hero, following the events at Harpers Ferry. By the middle 1850s Emerson was a publicly committed abolitionist; by the late 1850s he showed no reluctance to engage in the public fray; and by the start of the War he categorically rejected the South. In the early 1860s he supported the cause of the Union with all the patriotic fervor which swept the North.[16]

The development of his public posture on the slavery question is at once uncharacteristic and understandable. Once Emerson recognized that what he and the country were hearing was not a "popgun" but the thunder of moral imperative, he acted. Rather than being merely apathetic or insulated from the public issues by the walls of an ivory tower, Emerson was an observer of the contemporary scene who simply refused to be ignited by the transitory concerns of his age. However, when he saw that public questions such as black slavery were crucial, he acted with the same determination which had led him to confront his audience at the Divinity School in the late 1830s. And given the unpopularity of the abolition cause even in the North, he exhibited the same sort of courage on the public platform as he had when facing the academy and clergy.

Amid his growing recognition that he was aging and his sense that his intellectual life was declining, Emerson toward the end of 1860 published *The Conduct of Life,* his third collection of fresh essays which, like its predecessors of the early 1840s, was drawn from his lectures. But as might be expected the years of the Civil War were taken up with an even closer attention to public affairs than he had demonstrated during the 1850s; he was still, however, principally a literary man and country squire. There was some lecturing, even a full circuit during the winter of 1863 which brought him as far west as Chicago and Milwaukee on the shores of Lake Michigan. As with most Americans, however, the War frequently dominated his consciousness, and he displayed a patriotism which, quite frankly, would have been inconceivable a few decades earlier. Although he was often unsure or ambivalent about Lincoln's administration, he was so caught up in the times that he shared his countrymen's grief as they mourned the assassinated president in the spring of 1865.

As was true for many intellectuals, the aftermath of the War was a period of some disillusionment for Emerson. He was disenchanted by the business-as-usual attitude which he saw prevailing as America's commercial community crashed on to continue the industrial and urban revolutions which had begun during the Jacksonian period. In this postwar period Emerson opposed many of the policies of the Reconstruction era and remained adamant in supporting the rights of the emancipated slaves.

In 1866 he published his second collection of poems, *May-Day and Other Pieces,* but the need for money required his again striking out on the lecture circuit of the West early in 1866; at the same time, now in his early sixties, he began to enjoy some of the pleasures and honors of old age. His daughter Edith gave him his first grandchild and Harvard, where he had been virtually persona non grata for three decades, conferred the Doctor of Laws degree on him in 1866. The fences with his alma mater continued to mend in these later years; in 1867 he was elected an Overseer and gave his second Phi Beta Kappa speech, thirty years after he had delivered "The American Scholar." He was a conscientious trustee, a supporter of President Eliot's liberalizing elective system, and even took up the demanding schedule of offering a series of eighteen lectures at the College in the space of about five weeks during the spring of 1870, a series he did not quite complete. A year later he was near the conclusion of another series at Harvard when he accepted an invitation to travel by rail to California, a trip he thoroughly enjoyed. The two lecture series in Cambridge were preceded by the publication of *Society and Solitude* (1870), a gathering which posed no small amount of difficulty for him in its preparation.

By the early 1870s Emerson's health had begun to fail and his memory continued on the decline which had begun in the late 1860s. And so, despite the pressure he was receiving from his publisher to complete *Parnassus,* a collection of favorite poems by other authors, and the trauma of a fire which had severely damaged his house in Concord, Emerson and his daughter Ellen boarded the steamer for Liverpool late in 1872 for what was to be his third and last trip to the Old World. In London he visited his old friend Carlyle, after which he and Ellen stopped in Paris on their way to the Mediterranean. After working their way through Italy, they were in Alexandria on Christmas Day and proceeded to Cairo, where they commenced the highpoint of the journey, a trip on the Nile. Early in 1873 they retraced their steps through Italy and France and arrived in London to enjoy a remarkably full social calendar, at once tiring and pleasurable. And following visits to Oxford and Edinburgh, they took the steamer back across the Atlantic and landed in Boston just a few days after Emerson's seventieth birthday.

More robust than he had been before the journey—travel always agreed with him—and enjoying somewhat enhanced financial security—the result of wise investments—his loss of memory continued to plague him. Nevertheless, he pursued his duties as a Harvard Overseer, remained active in The Saturday Club, had the satisfaction of witnessing his son Edward's graduation from the Harvard Medical School and his marriage in 1874, and enjoyed Lidian's recently discovered social success; no longer withdrawn, she had become an adept public speaker.

Parnassus was finally published late in 1874, and a year later *Letters and Social Aims* appeared; however, it bore the heavy marks of his collaborators, Ellen and, especially, James Eliot Cabot, who was to become his biographer, editor, and literary executor. Shortly before his seventy-first birthday Emerson again addressed an assembly at the Harvard Divinity School, but his public-speaking career was soon to end. He had some hand in preparing *Selected Poems,* published in 1876, and there were some additional speaking engagements in the late 1870s. But twilight was falling. On April 27, 1882, a month prior to his seventy-ninth birthday, he died quietly in the Concord house which he had shared with his family for almost forty-seven years.

Chapter Two
The Buds Burst

On Sunday evening, July 15, 1838, Ralph Waldo Emerson had his most unequivocal confrontation with orthodoxy when he addressed the half-dozen seniors at the Harvard Divinity School. He had been invited to speak by the students, not the faculty, and found himself before a standing-room-only crowd of a few hundred in the chapel in Divinity Hall. Delivered fewer than two years after the publication of his first volume, *Nature,* and scarcely ten months following his Phi Beta Kappa Address ("The American Scholar") at Harvard, the "Divinity School Address" bursts out of the period of Emerson's most intense Transcendentalism.[1]

Following an eloquent if not poetic opening paragraph in which he sings the "mystery of nature [which] was never displayed more happily"—in its sensuality hardly a conventional or expected beginning, in light of the audience and occasion—Emerson celebrates the value of spontaneous, individual perception which is central to his thinking and declares that the "laws of the soul" which each person has access to "are out of time, out of space, and not subject to circumstance" (*CW,* I, 76–77). He develops his argument by announcing that "This sentiment [which all might experience] is divine and deifying. It is the beatitude of man. It makes him illimitable. Through it, the soul first knows itself. . . . by showing the fountain of all good to be in himself, and that he, equally with every man, is an inlet into the deeps of Reason" (*CW,* I, 79).

What Emerson was raising was a philosophical issue which clergymen, both orthodox and dissenting, had pondered and debated over the generations. By placing his faith in the spontaneous, intuitive faculties of Man, rather than in less emotional and personal means, he was joining the ranks of the "heretics" and "infidels" who had rocked the ship of ecclesiastical state since the very beginning of the Massachusetts Bay Colony: the Quakers, Antinomians, and Arminians who for more than two centuries had confronted the establishments of the Calvinist Congregational churches, as well as the Unitarians and other liberals of Emerson's day who were challenging modern orthodoxy. These were not reactionaries or even conservatives before whom Emerson was throwing down the gauntlet. They were the liberal Unitarians who had long since captured his alma mater, the Harvard Divinity School.

Although the evidence indicates that he was not trying to be vindictive[2] in any portion of the "Address," what he went on to say was in all likelihood more provocative to his listeners than his beginning. He rejected the view that modern Man is merely "an appendage, a nuisance" and also the belief that "Miracles, prophecy, poetry, the ideal life, the holy life, exist as ancient history merely" (*CW,* I, 80). The lesson of Jesus, who "belonged to the true race of prophets"(*CW,* I , 81), had been perverted by historical Christianity. Whereas Christ was "the only soul in history who has appreciated the worth of a man"(*CW,* I, 82), institutional Christianity has corrupted his faith. And so, "The Church seems to totter to its fall, almost all life extinct" (*CW,* I, 84). It is administered and represented by formalist preachers out of touch with their faith, themselves, and their congregations. Their preaching "comes out of the memory, and not out of the soul. . . historical Christianity destroys the power of preaching, by withdrawing it from the exploration of the moral nature of man" (*CW,* I, 87). In his long and eloquent conclusion, he admonishes the fledgling preachers "to go alone. . . to love God without mediator or veil. . . . cast behind you all conformity, and acquaint men at first hand with Deity" (*CW,* I, 90). The self-respect and self-reliance he was calling for were not, in reality, all that different from the spirit of democracy which was affecting American political, social, and economic institutions during the second quarter of the nineteenth century. They were born of the same spirit which culminated in the events of 1848 in Europe and pervades modern societies. And they were deeply personal. We can never fully comprehend all the causes or conditions, conscious and unconscious, which drove Emerson to challenge the orthodox that evening in Cambridge. Perhaps his antiauthoritarian stance was the result of other currents—some deep and powerful—such as his revulsion at his own father's harsh condemnation of the Antinomian heresies of Anne Hutchinson two centuries earlier.[3] Whatever the reasons Emerson took his stand.

His remarks at the Divinity School were broadcast quickly in the community and triggered a generally vituperous response, especially from the clergy. The uproar which followed resulted not only from what he had said but from his style and rhetorical strategies, which may well have been considered offensive by many in the assembly.[4] Although members of his family were visibly disturbed by his assessment of the Church and the alternatives he proposed, they supported him during the crisis which followed. He was stung by the press and assaulted continuously in the flurry of printed responses touched off by his remarks. Andrews Norton, Emerson's "Unitarian Pope" who had been retired from Harvard since 1830, issued *A Discourse on the Latest Form of Infidelity* in 1839, the most stinging rebuke from the establishment. But Emerson had gone to Concord shortly after giving the "Address" and remained silent. Having had his say, he stayed aloof from the fray and appeared not to be distressed.

The public response, however, did touch him personally, which may have caused him to present a quite different message a week later when he spoke at Dartmouth College.[5] But he would not reveal the depth of his feelings until "Uriel," published in the first collection of his poetry late in 1846. Here Emerson cast himself as "Uriel," an archetypal emblem of the rebellious intellect, and described his impression of the response of the faculty, "The stern old war-gods" who "shook their heads" at his "rash word" (*W,* IX, 14). Despite the ironic tone of the poem, it seems he was not entirely comfortable in the role of shaker of the establishment. Emerson probably revealed the "disruptive" nature of his position in this poem more than he had in the "Address" itself. If there is a "lapse" for Uriel, it is not a "repentance"; Emerson betrays the depth of his antipathy in the poem, and if he conceived of his role as similar to that of Moses, he saw that the people he might lead—figuratively, that is—probably would prefer their Egypt to the land he promised them; going to that Land of Milk and Honey might require their trading off the comfortable security offered by their institution.[6]

The individualism Emerson championed was perfectly in keeping with the vital, assertive, energetic, and strenuously democratic times he lived in. The independence he prized, however, and the men he looked for to actualize it, were of a different kind from those sought by ordinary citizens and by the politicians and the institutions they supported and lived by. Emerson's optimism was also different from that of his fellow Americans. Their faith was inspired by economic and geographical expansion, material prosperity, and the promise of continued growth. Whereas their conception was symbolized by the crowing braggart—half horse, half alligator, half man, as the river-men conceived him—Emerson's reality was that Man was "a god in ruins. . . . the dwarf of himself," as his orphic poet described him near the end of *Nature* (*CW*, I, 42). Addressing the Phi Beta Kappa Society at Harvard in 1837, he stated the case more pointedly when he complained that Man "has wronged himself. . . . [and] almost lost the light that can lead him back to his prerogatives. Men are become of no account" but are "bugs, are spawn, and are called 'the mass' and 'the herd'" (*CW*, I, 65). And the reason for this unrealized potential was in large measure the gross materialism of the times, the same money-grabbing, acquisition-crazed fever assailed by other Romantics such as Thoreau, Melville, and, though later in life, Whitman. In the same address, "The American Scholar," Emerson lamented his fellow citizens' confusing material well-being with the acquisition of "money or power" (*CW*, I, 65). This was the brutalizing, dehumanizing condition in American life which had to be, and could be, transcended. One early reviewer of *Nature* recognized the pertinence of Emerson's assessments of the country's conditions when he wrote: "In our own bustling country, where banks, steam boats and rail roads seem to engross the nation's attention, we are happy to find some spirits, who keep aloof from the vulgar melee, and in calm of soul, live for Nature and for God."[7] In similar fashion, the English critic Richard Monckton Milnes considered the "Idealistic Pantheism" in *Nature* to be the natural and healthful outgrowth of a society which, prizing "self-important pomp and tumult," nurtured Americans who suffered from "outraged sensibilities, blasted hopes, and thwarted affections"[8]—outraged, blasted, and thwarted precisely because of a poverty of outlook. As a remedy, or at least alternative, Emerson offered his Transcendental vision.

The essential principles of his Transcendental credo were announced with candor in *Nature* and then were echoed and amplified in "The American Scholar" and the "Divinity School Address." Let us focus on some of the key assertions Emerson made, the themes he sounded in these early writings: the importance of the Present; Idealism; the use of

Reason to transcend; and individualism. Along the way, we will also consider some aspects of the styles and rhetorical strategies he employed.

Nature, composed of an introduction and eight chapters, commences with his observation that modern Man is crippled by an inordinate and unnecessary reverence for the past and with a bold announcement of the rights and prerogatives every human being should enjoy. Like "foregoing generations" each age should behold "God and nature face to face." Why must we build "sepulchres of the fathers" and "grope among the dry bones of the past" (*CW,* I, 7)? His estimate of the past supplies the foundation on which many of his views are constructed. It is important to understand that in dismissing history Emerson was not simplistic, or even whimsical. He was not merely playing out an intellectual, emotional, and cultural Oedipal drama, asserting in the phrase of one recent critic a "secular incarnation" of the self.[9] His response to the past and his view of history were more subtle and sophisticated—in a word, transhistorical. In fact, Emerson's wrestling with the question is in the tradition established by the very nature of the Protestant Reformation. Just as his forebears had created rather than rectified history, Emerson was attempting to replace historical tradition and institutional authority with private judgment. He and his fellow Transcendentalists, Protestants in the extreme, were preoccupied with releasing Man's spiritual and moral life from history and placing the burden of responsibility upon the individual.[10]

A year later, in "The American Scholar" oration, Emerson was to assert the Present even more vigorously. Discussing the great influences to which the scholar is exposed, he identifies "the mind of the Past,—in whatever form, whether of literature, of art, of institutions, that mind is inscribed. Books are the best type of the influence of the past" (*CW,* I, 55). But he cautions that "Each age . . . must write its own books; or rather, each generation for the next succeeding" for "Instantly, the book becomes noxious. The guide is a tyrant" (*CW,* I, 56). If an age fails to use books properly, it will produce not "Man Thinking" (the present participle suggests original, vital engagement) but mere "thinkers"—"bookworm[s]," "bibliomaniacs"—unhealthy "men of talent . . . who set out from accepted dogmas, not from their own sight of principles." Cicero, Locke, Bacon, and others whose shadows loom so heavily through history were, he insists, "only young men in libraries when they wrote these books" (*CW*, I, 56). What Emerson seeks to avoid is the fettering of creative genius by a servile reverence for the past, the tradition. When he cries that "The book, the college, the school of art, the institution of any kind, stop with some past utterance of genius" and insists that "They look backward" whereas "genius always looks forward" (*CW*, I, 57), he is in fact addressing himself to a dilemma American colonials and early nationals had grappled with for almost two centuries. Indeed, what relationship were America's institutions and mores to have to those of the parent European culture, particularly England's? How free of the conventions of conduct was the American to be? These and related questions had been debated with mounting intensity, especially by literary intellectuals, at least from the time of the Revolution some sixty years earlier.

One sensible way of appreciating what Emerson says when he asserts the primacy of the present and champions modern Man unfettered by inhibiting and stultifying traditions, is to place his vigorous nationalism in the context of the rapidly maturing social and political independence which was developing in the fledgling republic. This is not to apologize for or defend what some readers may interpret as cultural and intellectual arrogance. Rather, it is to suggest that in questioning the viability of the past, Emerson expressed the chauvinism shared in varying degrees by all American nationalists of the period. His point and strategy are succinctly expressed halfway through his discussion of the influence of the past on the scholar, when he insists that "Genius is always sufficiently the enemy of genius by over-influence." Arguing that the literature of the past, for example, must be "sternly subordinated" by "Man Thinking," he concludes that when the scholar "can read God directly, the hour is too precious to be wasted in other men's transcripts of their readings." Books are not only "for the scholar's idle times" (*CW*, I, 57) but when taken up must be used correctly. To be genuinely original the scholar must eschew convention, tradition, imitation; similarly, he must avoid the provincialism of nationalism as skillfully as he would refuse to be a mere repeater of others' opinions, whether those others are of today or of the past.[11]

In four of the early chapters of *Nature* ("Commodity," "Beauty," "Language," and "Discipline"), after he has asserted the centrality of the present by placing it in proper perspective vis-à-vis the past, the tradition, he defines the ends and methods of the Transcendental quest. He includes under commodity "all those advantages which our senses owe to nature," the benefit of which is *"temporary and mediate, not ultimate"* (*CW*, I, 11; my italics). But this "mercenary benefit" is merely the predicate from which spring the higher and more worthy uses of nature. He concludes the chapter with a vigorous and homely, aphoristic phrasing: "A man is fed, not that he may be fed, but that he may work" (*CW*, I, 12).

Beyond materialism lies "A nobler want of man . . . served by nature, namely, the love of Beauty" (*CW*, I, 12), which is the subject of *Nature*'s third chapter. He discusses three aspects of Beauty, claiming, first of all, that "the simple perception of natural forms is a delight" (*CW*, I, 13). Properly understood, however, "this beauty of Nature which is seen and felt as beauty, is the least part. The shows of day . . . become shows merely, and mock us with their unreality" when we become aware of the second aspect of Beauty: "The presence of a higher, namely, of the spiritual element is essential to its perfection. . . . Beauty is the mark God sets upon virtue" (*CW*, I, 14–15). Finally, Emerson argues for Beauty as "an object of the intellect" which "searches out the absolute order of things as they stand in the mind of God, and without the colors of affection" (*CW*, I, 16).

He presents one of his most forceful and memorable expressions of the Idealist posture in Chapter 4, "Language." Joining Commodity and Beauty, Language is "A third use which Nature subserves to man" (*CW*, I, 17). He uses the clearest, most tested rhetorical technique and begins by listing the three dimensions he will explore in the chapter:

1. Words are *signs* of natural facts.
2. Particular natural facts are *symbols* of particular spiritual facts.
3. Nature is the *symbol* of spirit.
   (*CW*, I, 17; my italics)

The correspondences between and among the dimensions he explores articulate this essential Idealism, his fundamental premise that all things possess resonances of meaning and significance which Man, if he is properly engaging them, must strive to reach.

Arranging his material climactically, Emerson begins by stating that "Every word which is used to express a moral or intellectual fact, if traced to its root, is found to be borrowed from some material appearance. *Right* originally means *straight; wrong* means *twisted,*" and so forth. In regard to the possibility of our grasping the unadorned truth in the simplicity of "root," primitive contexts, however, he notes that the "process . . . is hidden from us in the remote time"(*CW,* I, 18; Emerson's italics).

It is in his explication of the second assertion about the symbolic that Emerson begins to explore the full implications of his meanings. He leaves his brief consideration of the origin of all words and proclaims that "it is things which are emblematic. Every natural fact is a symbol of some spiritual fact" (*CW,* I, 18). Seeking greater clarity, he once again brings us back to the unblemished, prelapsarian world for a glimpse at the concrete imagery of the uncorrupted primitive; he drives home the point in a passage remarkable for its vividness and directness, when he insists that "The world is emblematic." Alluding to Swedenborg, he concludes that " 'The visible world and the relation of its parts, is the dial plate of the invisible' " (*CW,* I, 21). What Emerson is doing is returning to the Universe the spiritual dimension which he and his fellow Transcendentalists felt it had been robbed of by the sterile, linear logic of eighteenth-century rationalism. To restore the spiritual he insists that the "cosmological dualism of the Platonic tradition" be retained, and that polarities such as worldly and other-worldly, lower and higher, be restored.[12]

If indeed the "world *is* emblematic" (my italics) and a prior generation's manipulation of the "dial plate" probably will have limited, or even scant influence on subsequent generations' turnings, by what means shall Man transcend? The answer to this question once again brings to the fore one of the more provocative aspects of Emerson's thought. He saw two basic avenues by which Man might approach the ultimate: one rational, the other nonrational. Using terminology which had long been conventional among philosophers and theologians (although it is not current today), he designated the rational as the "Understanding" and the nonrational as "Reason." For Emerson, Reason—the nonrational, the spontaneous—was the only method by which Man might transcend. Emerson's reliance on Reason, the higher faculty, served him well in his repudiation of Enlightenment mechanism; with it, correspondence between the natural and spiritual was a fact and transcendence a possibility.[13] On a more fundamental level it was a reaction, in fact, against the rigorous intellectual tradition in which he had been trained as an undergraduate at Harvard and then in the Divinity School and which was at the foundation of the Unitarian church he had served for a brief period.

Having distinguished between Nature and Soul in the fourth and last paragraph of his brief "Introduction" to *Nature*—"all that is separate from us, all which Philosophy distinguishes as the NOT ME, that is, both nature and art, all other men and *my own body,* must be ranked under this name, NATURE" (*CW,* I, 8; my italics)—Emerson continues to explore the relationship between the two. Near the end of the chapter on "Language" he had stated that "A Fact is the end or last issue of spirit" (*CW,* I, 22); and so he continues in Chapter 5, "Discipline," to argue that the NOT ME (that is, Nature) is educative of both the Reason and the Understanding. He begins with a discussion of the Understanding's relation to Nature: "Every property of matter is a school for the understanding,— its solidity or resistance, its inertia, its extension, its figure, its divisibility" (*CW,* I, 23). Then, working from the basic assumption that Man is an *analogist,* he argues that "All things are moral," that is, are suffused with the "moral law" (*CW,* I, 25–26).

In Chapter 6, "Idealism," he enlarges and clarifies his view. The world—Nature, the NOT ME—is an appearance perceived by the senses; but "If the Reason be stimulated to more earnest vision, outlines and surfaces become transparent, and are no longer seen." And so "Nature is made to conspire with spirit to emancipate us" (*CW,* I, 30). Unfixing and opening the eye of Reason upon Nature, "The true philosopher and the true poet are one, and a beauty, which is truth, and a truth, which is beauty, is the aim of both. . . . It is, in both cases, that a spiritual life has been imparted to nature; that the solid seeming block of matter has been pervaded and dissolved by a thought" (*CW,* I, 34). The ultimate example, of course, is Shakespeare.

It is within these contexts that we must consider one of Emerson's most important, stunning, and controversial passages: the "transparent eye-ball" section in the fourth paragraph of Chapter 1. He writes:

Crossing a bare common, in snow puddles, at twilight, under a clouded sky, without having in my thoughts any occurrence of special good fortune, I have enjoyed a perfect exhilaration. Almost I fear to think how glad I am. In the woods too, a man casts off his years, as the snake his slough, and at what period soever of life, is always a child. In the woods, is perpetual youth. Within these plantations of God, a decorum and sanctity reign, a perennial festival is dressed, and the guest sees not how he should tire of them in a thousand years. *In the woods, we return to reason and faith.* There I feel that nothing can befal me in life,—no disgrace, no calamity, (leaving me my eyes,) which nature cannot repair. *Standing on the bare ground,*—my head bathed by the blithe air, and uplifted into infinite space,—*all mean egotism vanishes. I become a transparent eye-ball. I am nothing. I see all. The currents of the Universal Being circulate through me; I am part or particle of God.*

(*CW,* I, 10; my italics)

Inevitably, the question arises whether Emerson was recording a mystical experience he himself had undergone. Of course, we can never be certain if he did or did not. But it appears that he did not.[14] In any case, the passage is of less interest and significance for its possible autobiographical resonances than for its substance and style.

The progression Emerson offers—from the "bare common," through his "perfect exhilaration" and to his "fear to think how glad" he is—is followed by his metaphor of development, the snake casting off his slough. In turn he celebrates childhood, youth, and communion with nature, then touches upon the religious dimensions of the experience, and concludes on the hopeful note that there is "no disgrace, no calamity . . . which nature cannot repair." There follows the compressed restatement which commences by bringing us down to earth again to observe the speaker "Standing on the bare ground," yet with his "head bathed by the blithe air, and uplifted into infinite space." Without preparation, without warning, virtually simultaneously in one sentence we soar from earth to "infinite space." The passage is concluded by six rather breathless, ecstatic utterances—clauses—which announce his dissolved "egotism" and nothingness, his transition to seer, and his merger with the Deity. The entire process is captured succinctly and beautifully in the "transparent eye-ball" image: the reporter or speaker is so thoroughly merged at the moment of transcendence that he is indistinguishable from his environment; he is an "eye-ball"—not merely an eye, concrete and, above all, functional—the means, in fact, to vision. In their brevity these are the utterances of poetic prose which if cast upon a page in the fashion of conventional English poetry are close to the short, rich line Emerson favored. Equally important is the absence of linear, logical progression. With the poet we are swept up in the moment of transcendence; we soar from the finite to the infinite in the space of a few words.

Perhaps it is this very absence of rational progression—in the experience he describes and in the style he employs—which is at the heart of the difficulty many readers have with this passage and with Emerson's writing generally. One of the oldest and most-worn saws in Emerson criticism is that his essential unit was the sentence. Distinguished critics over the past century and a half have voiced this concern. In her review of Emerson's *Essays: Second Series* in 1844, Margaret Fuller, his close friend, complained that "Single passages and sentences engage our attention too much in proportion. These essays, it has been justly said, tire like a string of mosaics or a house built of medals."[15] And among the host of critics who have voiced similar discontent about the alleged lack of coherence, even unity, within, between, and among paragraphs as well as entire essays, there is F.O. Matthiessen; he claimed not only that the sentence was Emerson's unit but that he had a problem joining several into paragraphs, a difficulty, it is suggested, which is similar to that he confronted in attempting to reconcile the individual and society.[16] Perhaps the problem lies as much in the premises and expectations of his readers as it does in Emerson's prose. The reader who tries to find the passage's coherence by means of conventional, logical transitions—rational bridges—probably insures his disappointment as much as he would were he to prize and demand rational connections when confronting counterpoint in music, paradox in Renaissance literature, or the montage technique in art cinema. To do so would be to ignore the stylistic and structural assumptions and strategies upon which and according to which the artist has constructed his work.

The importance of style to the statement Emerson is making in this small passage signals its importance in the entire essay. To separate style from sense in our attempt to grasp the essay's meaning would in fact be an exercise in translating Emerson's rich if unconventional structures and artistic strategies into the pedestrian, if clear, rhetoric of conventional expository prose. While such a process might facilitate our comprehension of substance on an initial reading, if it is sustained it will compromise or even drain the work of its aesthetic richness. In brief, exposition engages the reader's "Understanding." But Emerson the artist sought to cultivate his reader's imagination at a higher, more integrated and richer level—on the plane, if you will, of the "Reason," the higher faculty.

There is no question that as a young man Emerson was drilled in the basic principles of rhetoric—including organization and structure—as they were set forth by period authorities such as Blair. It is, in fact, inconceivable that any young man exposed to the curricula of the Boston Latin School and Harvard College in the early nineteenth century could avoid gaining a thorough mastery of such basic principles of composition. The point seems to be that early in his career as a lecturer and author he discarded these conventions in favor of others which appeared to him more effective in reaching the audiences to whom he was speaking and for whom he was writing.[17] Recognizing Emerson's willingness to experiment in prose—whether spoken or written—is the first step the reader must take toward the end of appreciating his freshness. (Were I observing the conventions of logical transitions in exposition, I would alert the reader that we are returning to our discussion of *Nature*. In the Emersonian spirit, however, I will not.)

As Richard Lee Francis has suggested in a remarkably perceptive consideration of Emerson's "architectonics" in *Nature,* by 1836 the author had already abandoned the rigorous, conventional tradition of pulpit oratory and was striking out in new directions, incorporating alternative aesthetic strategies in his writing. On the level of exposition in *Nature,* Emerson explores the "uses" of nature and approaches his subject from the direction of Understanding. But the linear, analytical arrangement of chapters such as 4, on "Language," where he presents his materials in specific, objective terms, is counterpointed by companion chapters which are more personal or theoretical. The structure— that is, the architecture—of the entire book, rather than being a linear—rational—progression up a ladder, with appropriate logical transitions, is in fact a "mounting dialectic definition." When those chapters which are relatively specific and objective are paired with their more personal or theoretical mates—for example, the "Introduction" with Chapter 1, Chapter 2 with Chapter 3—we see them "in some sort of helixical evolutionary scheme." The whole is a "baroque progression" and in its arrangement, its architectonics, the essay is analogous to a baroque cantata; the more pedestrian chapters which explore matter are the counterparts of the recitatives; those which are concerned with mind—Emerson's overriding emphasis—are the counterparts of the more exciting chorales.[18] And so, the reader who insists upon what he may consider a more conventional exposition of the subject at hand will inevitably be as disappointed by Emerson's prose as the Realist Mark Twain was by Cooper's Romanticism.

Having explored "Commodity," "Beauty," and "Language" in Chapters 2 through 4, Emerson presents the facets of nature which educate the Understanding and the Reason in "Discipline," Chapter 5. He considers the ways we use to comprehend nature, intellectually arranging it by means of the Will; and then, moving to the higher plane of Reason, he discusses the morality of the universe: "Sensible objects. . . . hint or thunder to man the laws of right and wrong, and echo the Ten Commandments." So, "All things with which we deal, preach to us" (*CW*, I, 25–26). This morality is the predicate from which springs the Unity Man perceives amid the variety he observes in the forms and actions of nature. Of all creatures only Man can order nature and use it to comprehend himself and his place in the universe. In Chapter 7, "Spirit," one of the shortest in the essay, he discusses in greater detail the spiritual dimensions or significances of nature: "It suggests the absolute. . . . It is a great shadow pointing always to the sun behind us" (*CW*, I, 37). The better part of the chapter is devoted to exploring the fact that the world and Man himself proceed from the same Superior Being and that these are phenomena, not substances. In the exposition, Chapter 7 amplifies Chapter 5.

Chapter 6, "Idealism," is probably the bridge Emerson wrote to mend the "crack" he sensed in the book's structure.[19] Lest the reader miss the point he is emphasizing in the greater part of "Discipline" and in "Spirit"—the focus is on the uses and necessity of Reason—he offers one of the longest chapters in the essay. To demonstrate that Reason "mars this faith" in the "absolute existence of nature," that it adds "grace and expression" to the "sharp outlines and colored surfaces" of nature, Emerson emphasizes the dualism of the universe—the perceiving Me and the Not Me which is seen—and discusses the superior power of the poet such as Shakespeare to unfix things and so make them "revolve around the axis of his primary thought" (*CW*, I, 30–31). He amplifies by noting the similarities and differences between the poet and the philosopher who, unlike sensual people, impart spiritual life to nature. Finally, he argues that intellectual science fixes Man on Ideas, "immortal necessary uncreated natures," and as a result renders "our outward being . . . a dream and a shade" (*CW*, I, 34). Ideas allow Man to soar, to be renewed; and religion and ethics—the practice of ideas and the introduction of ideas into life—degrade nature and suggest its dependence on spirit. He concludes the transitional chapter with a summary and insists that the Ideal view of the world conforms to the Reason, "sees the world in God." All phenomena are "one vast picture, which God paints on the instant eternity, for the contemplation of the soul" (*CW*, I, 36).

The last of *Nature*'s eight chapters, "Prospects," reasserts the limitations of empirical science, arguing that while it classifies, it fails to address itself to the ultimate question of the unity of creation. Science, on the level of the Understanding, offers "half-sight" (*CW*, I, 41). Emerson's faith is in Plato's dictum: " 'poetry comes nearer to vital truth than history' " (*CW*, I, 41) or, for that matter, any of the conventional avenues by which Man pursues the ultimates. Following his presentation of the bard's orphic sayings, aphoristic utterances which are the upshot of vision, the opening of Reason's eye, Emerson finally reaffirms his abiding faith in the individual and points out that when prepared the mind will reveal its wisdom by seeing the miraculous in the commonplace. Since it is possible for each of us to see the world with new eyes, he virtually demands that each man "Build, therefore, your own world" (*CW*, I, 45).

Emerson amplified and applied some of the essential tenets of the philosophy which he explored in *Nature* not only in the "Divinity School Address" but also in "The American Scholar." His requirements that the scholar embrace the present and use the past only after placing it in perspective are analogous to his demand in *Nature* that Man use his Reason rather than his Understanding. In the opening section of "The American Scholar" he insists on Reason over Understanding, "Man Thinking" (*CW*, I, 56) rather than the mere thinker. The two center sections of the Address concern the influences on the scholar and then his duties. While action is subordinate although essential, nature itself is the most important influence on the scholar. The scholar must confront nature as freely and freshly as he does his reading. Gradually, he will perceive the unity underlying phenomena. And ultimately, "whatsoever new verdict Reason from her inviolable seat pronounces on

the passing men and events of to-day,—this he shall hear and promul-
gate." In full self-confidence he must never defer "to the popular cry" or
"quit his belief that a popgun is a popgun, though the ancient and
honorable of the earth affirm it to be the crack of doom." His must be a
"free and brave" (*CW,* I, 63) self-trust inspired by Reason.

"The American Scholar" is frequently alluded to as America's "intellectual Declaration of Independence."[20] But it was also a deeply personal
statement which developed from and expressed Emerson's "troubled
thinking about his own role as scholar" in the mid-1830s.[21]
Having left the ministry earlier in the decade, he was forced to create
his own profession during the 1830s. But he was not alone. The
movement to separate church and state by the mechanism of disestab-
lishment, initiated by Jefferson and his followers a half-century before,
had finally reached Massachusetts, the last state to pass such legislation,
in 1831. Although we must never forget that Emerson in effect disestab-
lished himself, we must also recognize that the "problem of vocation"
he confronted was a dilemma he shared with numerous other ex-
ministers who were cut loose from their comfortable clerical moorings
in the period. These were young men trained by a system which
functioned according to assumptions that were fast-dissolving as
American culture became secularized, industrialized, and urbanized.[22]
For Emerson the question was more pointed than it was for the vast
majority of his contemporaries. Was he to be an actor or a scholar, an
active reformer or an observer? We have already discussed his rejection
before 1850 of the active role of reformer, for example. The fundamental
issue "The American Scholar" set forth for both Emerson and his
audience concerned the creativity and originality of the scholar. The
clarification of his view, his answer, had not been easy. As has been
demonstrated, it developed through several stages, from a notion of the
scholar as a mere "watcher," a detached observer, in 1833–34, to the
position he states so eloquently in "The American Scholar" itself. The
gravity of the problem is perhaps best illustrated by the fact that better
than a third of "The American Scholar" is traceable to passages in his
journals and lectures.[23] Rightly understood, any reading of the Address
should emphasize the personal nature of his description of the scholar, as
well as call attention to his plea for literary nationalism; the Phi Beta
Kappa Address is equally as much an expression of a phase in Emerson's
struggle to find a satisfactory vocation and "to affirm a creed of self-

reliance" for himself and his listeners.[24] This is not to deny the importance of "The American Scholar" as a document in the young country's
quest for national identity but rather to place its call in proper
perspective.

In the fourth and concluding section of his speech Emerson extends
and applies to his audience of scholars—old and young—some of the
main conclusions of *Nature*. He welcomes the present "age of Revolution;
when the old and the new stand side by side, and admit of being
compared. . . . This time, like all times, is a very good one, if we but
know what to do with it." And he celebrates the new interest in the
commonplace of the present and the new recognition of the individual.
"Give me insight into to-day, and you may have the antique and future
worlds. . . . The meal in the firkin . . . the ballad in the street; the news
of the boat . . . show me the ultimate reason of these matters" and
Emerson will see that "one design unites and animates the farthest
pinnacle and the lowest trench" (*CW,* I, 67–68). There is also the faith of
the democrat who recognizes the importance and sanctity of each person,
where "slumbers the whole of Reason" (*CW,* I, 69). All this serves as the
prelude to the ringing "intellectual Declaration of Independence" with
which he concludes his challenge. American freemen, following their
best instincts, will cease being "timid, imitative, tame" and listening to
the "courtly muses of Europe. . . . A nation of men will for the first time
exist, because each believes himself inspired by the Divine Soul which
also inspires all men" (*CW,* I, 69–70).

The sensitive reader of this and similar passages in American letters of
the period cannot reduce them to simplistic, chauvinistic bellowings—
premature flexings of cultural muscle. The issues which underlay the
question Emerson and his contemporaries were asking about their culture's relation to the Old World's traditions had been debated for decades
and still entertain American intellectuals in the twentieth century.
Naturally, there were and are no simple, generally accepted answers to
such queries. In Emerson's day there were relatively conservative
spokesmen, on the one hand, figures such as Irving and, later, Hawthorne, and there were radical people, on the other, New Yorkers such as
Evert Duyckinck and Cornelius Mathews and their whole Young
America movement during the 1840s, and Whitman in the 1850s. The
issues Emerson and his contemporaries were speaking to were complex,
multi-layered, and knotty, packed with political, sociological, and artis-

tic implications. And as is always the case when a culture engages in a dialogue which is crucial to its values and future, some spokesmen must take extreme positions, if only to clarify the questions. The call for an autochthonous literature which Emerson and others made was intimately connected to the Transcendentalists' insistence that the contemporary American had as much possibility for access to the Divine Mind as any other person in another culture at any time. For Emerson the issue of nationalism was closely tied to that of individualism. And in his answer he was lending to his American scholar the promise and dignity which were required to rescue him and the culture from the debasement of colonialism. Fresh and original energies and engagement were crucial not only for the clergy and the observer of nature, but for the scholar, particularly Emerson.

Chapter Three

Self-Evolving Circle

Essays: First Series (1841), like its counterpart which was to appear three years later, is not a random collection of commentaries on various subjects but rather a unified and coherent exploration of the key facets of Emerson's thought during the five years after the publication of *Nature* in 1836. This quality of the volume is frequently missed since most readers treat the essays as separate entities, often because they encounter them in anthologies and other samplers. Even more disturbing, some readers approach Emerson with the expectation that his thought is simply not systematic. Perhaps this latter expectation arises from the conventional wisdom discussed in the preceding chapter, the truism that Emerson's unit is the sentence and occasionally the paragraph, and that his writing fails in its larger units. "History," the lead piece in the first volume of *Essays,* contradicts these assumptions, these expectations.

At the heart of "History" are the preciousness and centrality of the individual which Emerson sang in the earlier prose and which he brings to a crescendo in the brilliant "Self-Reliance," the second essay in this first collection. Rather than springing upon the reader with another vigorous and bold celebration of Man's worth, he begins his first collection of essays with an exploration of the modern age's various connections with historical Man and history in general. Just as he had in *Nature,* he begins at the beginning—the past.

Opening with the Transcendental truth that "There is one mind common to all individual men. Every man is an inlet to the same and to all of the same" (*CW,* II, 3), he proceeds to insist upon the all-too-often ignored value of the present—the now—vis-à-vis the past, the historical. "Of the universal mind each individual man is one more incarnation" (*CW,* II, 4), at least equal to and in fact ultimately more important than other incarnations, earlier and contemporary. His focus on the significance and worth of history here in the first of his essays is not only appropriate but, in terms of the collection's coherence, mandatory. It is appropriate in light of his and his culture's concern about their relationship to the European heritage from which they had sprung: on the one hand, their constant and almost universal obsession with defining their ties to the historical, parent culture; on the other, their youthful, rebellious, and enthusiastic assertions of freedom from it, their need for a cultural and intellectual independence to complement the political liberty Americans had gained scarcely a half-century before.

Further challenging the categories into which people are willing to freeze history, and so be dominated by it, Emerson asserts the subjectivity of history, if not its arbitrary qualities, and refuses to give it value as fact. Instead, it is "immortal sign," symbol—even, quoting Napoleon, " 'a fable agreed upon' " (*CW,* II, 6). Concluding that "there is properly no History; only Biography" (*CW,* II, 6), he drives home his point by merging his notions of the centrality of the individual confronting history and its very subjectivity. The beginning of the tenth paragraph summarizes matters nicely: "All inquiry into antiquity . . . is the desire to do away this wild, savage and preposterous There or Then, and introduce in its place the Here and the Now" (*CW,* II, 7). The next several paragraphs offer cogent illustrations of this point and, even more vigorously, of the inevitable subjectivity of various approaches and versions of historical reality. Under such circumstances how can any individual submit to the tyranny of another's perceptions? The beauty of Genius is that it does not submit to this locking of categories but insists on penetrating reality for itself; that is, Genius can recognize that "Nature is an endless combination and repetition of a very few laws. She hums the old well known air through innumerable variations" (*CW,* II, 9).

Emerson's concern about the abiding unity each person must seek among reality's varied manifestations occupies the next major segment of the essay. To develop his point he draws on illustrations from a range of intellectual and academic historical disciplines: civil and natural history, art and literature, and architecture. Just as "all public facts are to be individualized, all private facts are to be generalized" (*CW,* II, 12). Through all this discussion, he returns to the centrality of the mind of Self and brings it into even sharper focus in the series of analogies he draws between our interest in various epochs, an interest predicated upon their metaphoric significance to the ages of each individual: each person experiences his own Greek period, his own age of chivalry, and so forth. Even an individual's protest against the absurdities of his milieu has its counterpart in social reformation. Fables recount for us our own experience. Man must use facts, never be dominated by them—especially historical facts. Each of us is eternally at the center, "a bundle of relations, a knot of roots, whose flower and fruitage is the world" (*CW*, II, 20). The promise history holds forth is that each person passes "through the whole cycle of experience" and as he does collects "into a focus the rays of nature." And so history, "no longer . . . a dull book. . . . shall walk incarnate in every just and wise man" (*CW*, II, 21–22).

The penultimate paragraph launches an embittered, almost despondent attack on the conventional writing of history, and the essay concludes with the imperative that "Broader and deeper we must write our annals . . . if we would truelier express our central and wide-related nature, instead of this old chronology of selfishness and pride to which we have too long lent our eyes." Discarding fact and embracing symbol, we must penetrate nature not by the "path of science and of letters." Rather, we should be guided by "The idiot, the Indian, the child, and unschooled farmer's boy [who] stand nearer to the light by which nature is to be read, than the dissector or the antiquary" (*CW*, II, 23).

The reader who is conversant only with such early works as *Nature* and the two major addresses will hear familiar themes in "History": the centrality of Man and nature; the transiency and fluidity—therefore, the ultimate mutability—of the perceptions and categories of any man, system, or civilization; and, of course, the primacy of the Here and Now. These are not terribly radical insistences for a sophisticated and widely read intellectual in his late thirties. They are observations one might reasonably expect from a man of independent mind who appreciates scholarly prudence and caution. Equally important, though, in "History," as in the entire collection, Emerson is not merely serving up warmed-over and well-worn philosophy, materials he had used in his earlier statements. He is dwelling with greater leisure on various aspects of earlier, basic insights and more fully exploring them and their corollaries; he is pushing through to new avenues of speculation, entertaining the intricacies and implications of their various effects. As we have seen, his fundamental quarrel is with the authority of institutions and dogmas, in this case those of the past, over the moral authority of the individual's own intuitions. Moral and spiritual reality, the crucial ends of any person's life, are "transhistorical."[1]

Having challenged the tyranny of the past, Emerson sets out in the second piece in the collection, "Self-Reliance," to explore the implications of the fierce individualism at the heart of his Transcendental faith. "Self-Reliance" will continue to enjoy its place as one of the half dozen most moving Emersonian statements for as long as he is read. Radical in the extreme, sometimes misinterpreted as an adolescent rejection of the social/political heritage and cultural tradition, it has been wrenched out of context by some enthusiasts or opportunists to serve as a literary and philosophical justification for puerile, whimsical behavior and half-baked rebellion. Rightly understood, however, it is a dramatic and persuasive expression of one of the essential articles of faith of Emerson the Transcendentalist: the dignity, the ultimate sanctity, of each human being. Perhaps one might better comprehend its significance and motive force by recalling the assertions of the common man which we have already seen were at the core of Jacksonian Democracy. "Self-Reliance" was composed toward the close of the Van Buren administration, which had been born in 1837 with the radicalism of the Loco Focos. The defiant independence Emerson announces and dwells upon in the essay might be better appreciated in comparison to other flexings and demonstrations of personal and cultural might in the America of the 1830s and 1840s.

Shifting his focus from history—the subject of the first piece in the collection—to the individual, Emerson dismisses the burden of the past in almost summary fashion halfway through "Self-Reliance": "The centuries are conspirators against the sanity and authority of the soul. . . . but the soul is light; where it is, is day; where it was, is night; and history is an impertinence and an injury, if it be anything more than a cheerful apologue or parable of my being and becoming" (*CW,* II, 38). The vigor of this passage derives from the vividness of the metaphor with which it begins, the compressed poetic structure of its center, and the outraged tone of its conclusion. He disposes of the past and concentrates our attention on his subject: the centrality and sanctity of the Self. What he is about here is close to prophecy. His intention is not to argue but to announce, not to analyze but to report Transcendental truth: "*Whim.* I hope it is somewhat better than whim at last, but. . . . Expect me not to show cause why I seek or why I exclude company" (*CW,* II, 30).

From the very first paragraphs of "Self-Reliance" he insists upon the primacy of Man: "believe your own thought," "Speak your latent conviction," be guided by "spontaneous impression," "imitation is suicide," "Trust thyself" (*CW,* II, 27–28). To justify these insistences he holds up as pristine models the "behavior of children, babes and even brutes"; the "nonchalance of boys. . . . independent, irresponsible" will lead to a more "genuine verdict" than the deliberation of the ordinary person who has been "clapped into jail by his consciousness." The result, Emerson promises, of this "unaffected, unbiased, unbribable, unaffrighted innocence, must always be formidable" (*CW,* II, 28–29).

He then shifts his attention to the adversary, the inhibitor of his ideal Romantic innocent: "Society everywhere is in conspiracy against the manhood of every one of its members. . . . Self-reliance is its aversion. It loves not realities and creators, but names and customs." And he concludes with the categorical insistence that "Whoso would be a man must be a nonconformist" (*CW,* II, 29). The call to confrontation we hear in this passage, the measured defiance of the motives that drive people to weave the social fabric and the rational, cynical description of the political organization, are similar to the cool, reasoned, and prodding tone we encounter in Thoreau's "Civil Disobedience" and countless other documents born of the reform and protest movements in progress in period America.

Emerson next concentrates on the Self, the individual, the potential victim and, hopefully, the antagonist of these forces which demand conformity. "Nothing is at last sacred but the integrity of your own mind" is an assertion pregnant with meaning for the Transcendentalist. Because Man is "sacred"—holy, the vessel of the Spirit—he must not "capitulate to badges and names, to large societies and dead institutions" (*CW,* II, 30). He must even be free of the philanthropies insisted upon by society—"miscellaneous popular charities; the education at college of fools . . . alms to sots; and the thousandfold Relief Societies." Each individual must be independent of all institutions; conformity to their usages "scatters your force." The path to freedom will not be easy, he warns, for Emerson refuses to live physically isolated, an outcast: "the great man is he who in the midst of the crowd keeps with perfect sweetness the independence of solitude" (*CW*, II, 31).

Reaching inward to focus on "The other terror that scares us from self-trust," Emerson demands fluidity, flexibility of character: "A foolish consistency is the hobgoblin of little minds, adored by little statesmen and philosophers and divines" (*CW*, II, 33). And after a few paragraphs of amplification in which he dwells upon human character and insists upon a variety of actions, he concludes, "I hope in these days we have heard the last of conformity and consistency." Insisting on his own stature, he refuses to defer to the "great man" who arrives for dinner. No person should ever "bow and apologize." Man must "affront and reprimand the smooth mediocrity and squalid contentment of the times, and hurl in the face of custom, and trade, and office, the fact which is the upshot of all history, that there is a great responsible Thinker and Actor working wherever a man works; that a true man belongs to no other time or place, but is the centre of things" (*CW*, II, 35). He drives home the command at the start of the next paragraph in a restrained, simple, imperative statement: "Let a man then know his worth." The point is illustrated by the homely parable of the drunken sot who is persuaded that he is a duke, a story which "owes its popularity to the fact, that it symbolizes so well the state of man, who is in the world a sort of sot, but now and then wakes up, exercises his reason, and finds himself a true prince" (*CW*, II, 36).

In a short paragraph he revives for a moment one of the major criticisms he had leveled in "The American Scholar," and in the first piece in the present collection, Man's deference to history, the past: "Our reading is mendicant and sycophantic" (*CW*, II, 36), unworthy of the possibilities of modern Man, especially the American freeman. And then in a longer section he ponders the source of Man's potential greatness, the spiritual center of all creation which is revealed to genius by means of "Spontaneity," "Instinct," "Intuition." Man is a medium who must only "allow a passage to its beams" (*CW*, II, 37) to enjoy the sanctity and wisdom of its truth which, by definition, does not lend itself to rational analysis. Emerson is no Pollyanna, however; he is warning that the divine insight he calls for is no easier to achieve than the nonconformity it will inspire.

The next major section of the essay is reminiscent of the indictments of modern Man which he had presented in earlier writings, notably in the last chapter of *Nature* where he had described Man as the "dwarf of himself." Here in "Self-Reliance" he complains that "Man is timid and apologetic; he is no longer upright; he dares not say 'I think,' 'I am,' but quotes some saint or sage" (*CW*, II, 38). The truth is evident but modern Man refuses to allow its passage, perhaps because of his mad desire for stability, his absurd insistence on certitude, and, finally, his avoidance of the "one fact the world hates, that the soul *becomes*" (*CW*, II, 40; Emerson's italics). Flux, relativity, evolution are the conditions of existence. Each of us must confront experience anew despite its uncertainties and insecurities. Modern Man must make his way in the world bearing the same questions and anxieties as Hawthorne's Robin in "My Kinsman, Major Molineux"; the promise, though, is that he too will "rise in the world" alone.[2]

Fulfillment is predicated upon the central assumption of Transcendental faith. Rather than wandering, searching for the reality in "the intruding rabble of men and books and institutions" (*CW*, II, 41), seek the God within. Tapping the source while in the loneliness of his nonconforming, ever-evolving isolation, modern Man will be elevated by the passage of its beams. And so each of us will achieve perfect freedom, pristine self-reliance.

Emerson is not implying that anyone in touch with the sources of his own virtue should impose his perception of the truth, his version of reality, on any other person. "If you are true, but not in the same truth with me, cleave to your companions; I will seek my own" (*CW*, II, 42). We shall all live in the truth as we understand it, however variously the ONE may manifest itself to us. This assertion is at the base of the relativism of Thoreau in "Civil Disobedience" and even *Walden*. It springs from perceptions similar to those of Melville's Ishmael—so different from the monomaniacal Ahab—who, near the end of Chapter 114 of *Moby-Dick*, "The Gilder," reflects: "There is no steady unretracing progress in this life; we do not advance through fixed gradations, and at the last one pause:—through infancy's unconscious spell, boyhood's thoughtless faith, adolescence' doubt (the common doom), then scepticism, then disbelief, resting at last in manhood's pondering repose of If. But once gone through, we trace the round again; and are infants, boys, and men, and Ifs eternally."[3]

Anticipating popular misinterpretations of such fierce individualism as "a rejection of all standard, and mere antinomianism" (*CW*, II, 42), Emerson answers the charge in the next paragraph by again insisting on his own integrity. He concludes this segment of the essay by returning to the demands of such self-reliance as he is championing, reiterates his critique of contemporary society, and celebrates the rewards to be gained by those who will abide by the self-trust he calls for.

The next major portion of the piece considers at some length the implications of the renovation—indeed, the revolution—he is demanding in matters such as religion, education, human pursuits, modes of living, associations, property, and even speculative views. As he expands, he weaves in arguments to support more vigorous nationalism and, in conventional Romantic terms, calls attention to some of the advantages enjoyed by primitive peoples, advantages which have been lost by civilized man. In a euphoric flight, he concludes with the injunction and promise that, "Nothing can bring you peace but yourself. Nothing can bring you peace but the triumph of principles" (*CW,* II, 51)—words which are central to the Transcendental visionary's challenge to the barbarous materialism of Jacksonian America.

In the most vigorous recent attack on Emersonian individualism, one critic suggests that such assertions, by Emerson and Americans generally, are to be viewed as Oedipal rejections of the fathers for their failures, which lead inevitably to an attempt to supplant paternal authority; in so doing, he argues, Emerson and his contemporaries, at least during the radical years of Jacksonian America, drifted toward an infantile "imperial separateness." Gathering all power to the Self, they discarded generations and history and, more practically, judged contemporary society irrelevant. They were, in short, subverting society.[4]

Perhaps the implications are not so dire. As we have seen, Emerson was not simplistically denying history but rather lifting the veil of its mystique in order to challenge its authority and even tyranny. Emersonian individualism was not merely a "morbid self-indulgence"[5] but rather a call for a self-reliance grounded in a sort of self-respect all too often not even contemplated by his contemporaries. In a period when democratic assertions about the value of the ordinary citizen were all too readily translated into crude narcissism and barbarous materialism, when the quest for national identity impelled a chauvinistical ahistoricism, Emerson was proclaiming a Transcendentalism which sprang from his abiding belief that each person could be in touch with the god within as well as with the divine currents of the universe. His was a profoundly religious message,[6] a call for a renaissance; it was not merely an attempt to transvalue or, at the most base level, subvert the religious impulse generally. In a more secular dimension his celebration of the individual was a warning and a challenge to each person not to be victimized by societal pressures to conform in a period of bandwagons, booms, and boosters which, he judged, were actually popguns.

In "History" and "Self-Reliance" Emerson concentrates on the individual's relations with his culture—culture in its broadest definition. In the next several essays he turns inward and works at a higher level of abstraction. "Compensation" and "Spiritual Laws" are, as he tells us in the sixth paragraph of the former, to be viewed as sacred "chapter[s]" in his consideration of those essential principles and laws which he judged to be at work in the universe and in Man's life.

"Compensation," one of Emerson's most provocative, even controversial, essays, articulates central Transcendental assumptions and principles which are frequently among the most difficult for modern readers to embrace. The essay is visionary and unrelenting in its announcements; but its optimism is probably less out of tune with modern intellectual thought than is its insistence that "All things are moral" (*CW*, II, 60). His foundation for this view is the notion of correspondence, the conception that the natural and spiritual worlds share the same law yet are also distinct. Since the end of the Transcendental quest is the perception of spiritual significance, to echo the language of *Nature*, Man is a connector, an analogist; when functioning properly he identifies the moral import of phenomena.[7] Secular philosophers, however, the witnesses to and products of the past century's explosion, have for the most part felt such conceptions to be unacceptable, largely because they seem out of tune with modern empiricism. The best and easiest way of grasping the Emersonian logic which gives rise to these assumptions is to follow his argument in the order he constructs it.

The first half-dozen paragraphs of "Compensation" challenge and dismiss vulgar, popular notions of the principle. Among other things, Emerson's concept does not allow that the virtuous will enjoy their reward in an afterlife, while the wicked enjoy the fruits of the earth. Such silliness, he notes, permeates the culture and is promulgated, for example, by leaders of institutionalized religion and even some literary men.

Emerson commences the exposition of his own view by asserting the "inevitable dualism" which "bisects nature." Man forever sees polarities: "each thing is a half, and suggests another thing to make it whole; as spirit, matter; man, woman; odd, even" and so forth. One of the essay's greatest strengths lies in the presentation of concrete, homely illustrations—mechanical forces, everyday life, and government—to demonstrate that "Whilst the world is thus dual, so is every one of its parts" (*CW*, II, 57). God is omnipresent. And here Emerson comes to one of the most controversial aspects of his thought: the necessary existence of evil in a universe permeated by the Deity. It is at this point that he insists on the morality of the universe. "Every act rewards itself," inevitably demands "retribution," and "integrates itself, in a twofold manner; first, in the thing, or, in real nature; and secondly, in the circumstance, or, in apparent nature." Yet even though the universe moves insistently toward unity, Man—and this is crucial—seeks to divide, "to act partially, to sunder, to appropriate" (*CW*, II, 60–61). For example, in their mania people seek greatness and foolishly trust that they will not be touched by bitterness; however, as fable, literature, history, law, mythology, proverbs, and the "sanctuary of the Intuitions" bear witness, tit will bring tat: "If you put a chain around the neck of a slave, the other end fastens itself around your own" (*CW*, II, 64).

It is at this juncture that Emerson speaks to another of the more controversial aspects of his thought, one which seems to contradict the intense claims for human freedom he made in pieces such as *Nature*, "The American Scholar," the "Divinity School Address," and even in the preceding essay, "Self-Reliance." There is a genuine fatalism or determinism in his insistence that "Our action is overmastered and characterized above our will by the law of nature" (*CW*, II, 64). He amplifies by considering once again the inevitable duality of life: first by dwelling on the necessary compensation, the punishment Man will suffer for the infractions of which he is guilty; then by exploring the principle at work in labor and the marketplace; and, finally, by moving to the opposite pole of "right action. Love, and you shall be loved" (*CW*, II, 68). The apparent fatalism, however, is somewhat qualified in "Spiritual Laws," where he works on a more abstract level to challenge some of the prevailing assumptions and conditions of his society such as the seeming inevitability of the frenetic and complicated, literally incomprehensible lives people lead—that German Confederacy, cited by Thoreau, whose borders not even a German can identify.[8] The predictable alternative he proposes, again anticipating his fellow Transcendentalist, is that we strive for "simplicty" and follow the "short ways" of nature (*CW,* II, 80). He rests finally in a vision of a harmonious society founded in uncompromising self-trust and mutual respect. These laws demand that Man turn inward and, at the same time, they determine that all teaching, all matters intellectual, cast aside masks to reveal reality. Emerson's major premise, again, is that the universe is moral. And insofar as Man is able to brush aside the encumbrances—the crazy-quilt of any culture's versions of absolute realities—he shall be in touch with nature and the spiritual reality which suffuses it. The degree to which each person is able to embrace this reality defines the degree to which he will have achieved his potential.

Another troublesome portion of "Compensation" arises when Emerson shifts his focus to what in effect is another exploration of evil. He argues that not only might defects become useful but that faults may carry the seeds of virtues, since "The soul *is* [Emerson's italics]. . . . real Being. Essence, or God" is ever at the center. It is the whole, not merely a part. Therefore, evil is by nature and definition privative, "the great Night or shade, on which, as a background, the living universe paints itself forth." He comes perilously close to the very lapse which he condemned earlier when he assures his readers in the next paragraph that although the "retribution due to evil acts" may not be evident to the Understanding, we may rest assured that the "eternal account" (*CW,* II, 70) will be called; he even insists that the threat hangs over the malign person by suggesting that he diminishes his own nature to the degree that he is evil.

The concluding five paragraphs of the essay are vigorously optimistic. Our "life is a progress" (*CW,* II, 71). Calamity is the necessary condition out of which new virtues shall appear. But the Almighty tells us life grows " 'Up and onward.' " Throughout he uses homely illustrations to demonstrate the persistent flow and flux of life and the universe, in the last paragraph even referring to personal pain and losses for which he himself has ultimately been compensated: "The death of a dear friend, wife, brother, lover, which seemed nothing but privation" but which "somewhat later assumes the aspect of a guide or genius" (*CW,* II, 73).

Here we have the most bothersome sort of Emersonian optimism. His position is scarcely rescued even by the suggestion that by means of his doctrine of compensation he is eschewing materialism,[9] ironically devaluating the term's marketplace currency by having traders in the spiritual employ it. Perhaps the real problem lies in compensation's having been cheapened by the Pollyannas of folk philosophy, the smooth purveyors of positive thinking who inevitably repel serious people attempting to manage the pain of experience. However sincere Emerson may have been in his attempt to comprehend life's misfortunes and tragedies, his stance nevertheless seems to be at odds with most serious modern thought, at least in the secular dimension.[10]

Less difficult to understand, though perhaps nonetheless trouble-some, is Emerson's concept of evil. Some of his critics complain that he lacks a "Vision of Evil," in Yeats's phrase, that he simply wants a "Tragic Sense," a mature appreciation of the "Power of Blackness." His optimism was best rejected by Melville when he commented on "Pru-dence," another essay in this first collection: "To one who has weathered Cape Horn as a common sailor, what stuff all this is." Newton Arvin has challenged such responses by suggesting that rather than averting his eyes from the contemplation of evil—suffering, frustration, moral evil, human malignity, depravity, and vice—Emerson views it from the perspective of Plato and the neo-Platonists, including Plotinus: evil is appearance—shadow—not reality.[11] However, Emerson's views on compensation and evil, as well as his optimism, are perhaps better understood as manifestations of his temperament rather than as the products of analysis—the illuminations of intuition, Reason, rather than of rational thought, Understanding.

Judging hastily from the next two titles, "Love" and "Friendship," one might anticipate that Emerson is further qualifying his bold assertions of individual independence. These two essays on basic human relationships are, in fact, vigorous explorations of the dangers of misuse and proper use of connections—to enhance independence. Both are examinations in the practical realm of the principles of freedom.

"Love" is a tightly arranged, circularly structured consideration of the potential effect of close human relations on individual freedom. But his point is that out of the regeneration born of connections with others and, of course, nature grows a genuine sense of Self, which supplies the foundation of a vigorous self-reliance. Rather than surrendering his liberty to the beloved, the lover finds that touching another enhances and insures his independence. More important, by loving another the lover grows, expands, proceeds outward and upward—from shadows to realities—in his search for "virtue and wisdom" (*CW*, II, 109). So what might appear as posing the threat to debase the individual spirit by immersing and drowning it in the waters of sensuality is, from the Transcendental vantage point, the springboard to progress toward greater freedom, a freedom arising from communion with reality. Rather than being compromised, the lover's independence is assured. The same sort of apparent paradox is implicit in the essay on "Friendship," a companion piece to "Love."

"Prudence" holds forth similar surprises. Essentially, the essay is a strong argument against conventional and base notions of the virtue. Although he acknowledges the necessary accommodations a sensible person must make in order to survive, Emerson condemns and laments the compromises demanded of the individual by a corrupt and fallen civilization, a culture which sees poets alienated and offers bogus recognition to men of talents—not genius—to scholars devoid of wisdom, for example. Rather than tempering his vigorous self-reliance with any substantial gesture toward the powers of the world, the pressures from without, Emerson steadfastly insists on the centrality and primacy of each person.

In the next short essay, "Heroism," he sustains his challenge to the forces which would compromise the individual. As Thoreau was later to lament the condition of those young men, his contemporaries, "who begin digging their graves as soon as they are born,"[12] so Emerson ponders the tragedy of the unrealized potentials, the corrupted purposes, of the "many extraordinary young men, who never ripened," who never, in a word, became heroes (*CW*, II, 153). In the battle against these corrupting forces, the hero must persist in order to preserve his integrity and sense of self, which are the results of his transcendence.

These four essays—"Love," "Friendship," "Prudence," and "Heroism"—are deeper probes into individualism which is probably the most important practical upshot of Emerson's Transcendental vision. Placed between "Compensation" and "Spiritual Laws"— speculations on some of the principles which form the foundation of individual freedom—on the one end, and "The Over-Soul" and "Circles" on the other, this group presents reinforcing, timely, and practical considerations of the necessity of each individual's right to insist on the primacy of the Self. Each person functions in his own present; life is a process; flux, change, and growth—the eternal upward spiral, the ever-widening circle—are the hallmarks of the world and of Man's development. These conditions of nature herself inevitably and rightly produce the "Imperial Self," if we understand the phrase in its proper, positive connotation.

"The Over-Soul," a detailed and at times lyrical exploration of the flow of divine wisdom into Man, offers a more thorough analysis of the process of revelation than Emerson had attempted in *Nature* or in the "Divinity School Address." He concentrates first on establishing the all-important premises that life and experience are in constant movement, never frozen; that touching reality is indeed rare, although it kindles the precious spark of hope which is crucial to each human being; and that "Man is a stream whose source is hidden. Our being is descending into us from we know not whence" (*CW*, II, 159). This exploration of the conditions necessary for Transcendental experience is reinforced by his dwelling on the "ethereal water" metaphor, the "flowing river, which . . . pours for a season its streams into me" and brings the "alien energy" from which "the visions come" (*CW*, II, 159–60). As in "Compensation" and "Spiritual Laws," the reader is confronted with the paradox of the Transcendental experience transforming passivity into liberty. Man may be free only after he quietly allows a passage to the divine spirit which Fate dictates will overcome him.

The spirit is succinctly described as "that Unity, that Over-Soul, within which every man's particular being is contained and made one with all other; that common heart . . . that overpowering reality" (*CW*, II, 160). While people ordinarily live apart—fragmented and uninspired—each of us has the potential to be integrated with the "whole," the "wise silence," the "ONE" (*CW*, II, 160) which suffuses all creation and to live in perfect harmony with it. Not merely an organ, function, faculty, intellect, or will, the human being is the temple in which resides all wisdom and good—light. From this light, this source, come genius, virtue, and love.

After using a series of illustrations to explore the reasons people fail to realize their potential as they bathe in the senses, Emerson shifts his attention to an extended discussion of the crucial concepts of the flow, evolution, and progress of the individual soul according to its own "law

of moral and of mental gain" (*CW,* II, 163). He insists that not only is
the spirit incarnated constantly in forms such as ours but that all beings
have the potential in various periods of life. The soul is not only the
"perceiver and revealer of truth"; its "communication of truth is the
highest event in nature, since it . . . passes into and becomes that man
whom it enlightens . . . takes him to itself" (*CW,* II, 166). Rather than
singing, reporting, and celebrating the Transcendental experience
itself—as he had, for example, in the "transparent eye-ball" passage in
Nature—in this essay Emerson turns his efforts more toward analyzing
it.

The remainder of the piece is devoted to an extended discussion and
celebration of this central Transcendental experience of *"Revelation,"*
this "influx of the Divine mind into our mind" which creates a "certain
enthusiasm," to use the term of the traditional theology Emerson
himself had rejected. His connotation for "enthusiasm" here is, of
course, positive. He welcomes the "insanity" (*CW,* II, 166–67) the
experience induces and proceeds to dwell upon its virtues and
benefits—for example, its democracy, its joys and exhilarations, its
inspiration to fierce individualism. He amplifies, describes, and, to the
degree he can, even analyzes, with a ringing application and exhorta-
tion: "Let man then learn the revelation of all nature, and all thought to
his heart; this, namely; that the Highest dwells with him; that the
sources of nature are in his own mind" (*CW,* II, 174). Finally, he refers
briefly to his conventional criticism of organized, institutionalized
Christianity, offers another euphoric description of Transcendental
merging, and concludes with an elevating, visionary announcement of
the powerful and sacred Self confronting the present and the future. In
its announcements as well as its cadences, the poetic prose of the latter
portion of the last paragraph anticipates the chants of Whitman in
"Song of Myself" a decade and a half later. The soul is "young, and
nimble. . . . not wise, but it sees through all things. . . . It is
innocent. It calls the light its own. . . . Behold, it saith, I am born
into the great, the universal mind. I the imperfect, adore my own
Perfect. . . . So come I to live in thoughts, and act with energies which
are immortal" (*CW,* II, 175).

It is important not to confuse Emerson's celebration of the nonrational processes here and elsewhere with antiintellectualism or to
understand it merely as signaling his rejection of the scientific spirit of

OUACHITA TECHNICAL COLLEGE

the modern age. He was reasonably well versed in a great deal of scientific thought, for example,[13] but was wary of the naturalist's penchant to function as a mere observer and classifier, and the scientist's willingness to believe his work is done when he freezes the categories. The naturalist must be a moral philosopher, not a mere recorder of phenomena. Observation and analysis, the provinces of the Understanding, could never inspire the exhilaration he describes in "The Over-Soul."

One of Emerson's most beautiful and elegant prose works, "Circles," is an eloquent presentation of some central, related tenets of Transcendental thought: flux, evolution, relativism, renewal. Life and experience are forever rebirths, mornings, springs. The image or symbol of the circle is at the center of the essay's successful rhetorical strategy. And Emerson concentrates our attention on it immediately in one of the most stunning pairs of sentences in his entire canon, the opening lines of the piece: "The eye is the first circle; the horizon which it forms is the second; and throughout nature this primary figure is repeated without end. It is the highest emblem in the cipher of the world" (*CW,* II, 179). In this dramatically compressed passage he draws together the central facts of all experience—the "Me" and the "Not Me," the subjective and the objective—establishes the preeminence and authority of the "I" as well as the "eye" (the pun is rich in suggestiveness), and introduces the metaphoric thread which binds together all creation and establishes its essential unity and coherence. As a number of readers have argued, the circle, by its very nature, suggests radiance, vitality, motion, and process and denies the static, the permanent, the circumscribed, and the finite. The figure hints at the "incessant creative energy of the World-Soul" and also serves as a "chief image . . . for a completed, integral, vital experience . . . an aesthetic act of seeing."[14] Not only can it reinforce the argument Emerson is making— one, as we shall see, which is crucial in his thought—the image can also illuminate the rhetorical strategy he is employing in the essay itself and even in the entire collection. For one reader it conjures up the suggestion of a radiating sunburst while for another it implies "aspiring circularity." Possibilities and processes rather than answers and solutions inform the structure as well as the sense of the essay.[15]

The initial four paragraphs lay down the principles whose manifestations he will explore. He immediately moves to the center of his argument by citing the authority of St. Augustine's description of the nature of the Deity as being "a circle whose centre was everywhere, and its circumference nowhere." The figure is perennially suggestive and has been used by philosophers and poets throughout the ages. The circle is the "first of forms" with immediate pertinence to "every human action. . . . Our life is an apprenticeship to the truth, that around every circle another can be drawn; that there is no end in nature, but every end is a beginning" (*CW*, II, 179). The close and reflective reader knows by the end of this first paragraph that Emerson is bringing him into a pointed explication of the predicate upon which he constructed the celebrations of the individual as well as of the present and future, "History" and "Self-Reliance," which begin *Essays: First Series.* Symbolically, the infinite series of concentric circles—perhaps best conceived of by imagining a stone dropped into the center of a shoreless body of water, suggesting a forever expanding universe—implies "the moral fact of the Unattainable, the flying Perfect" (*CW*, II, 179). Nothing is fixed, all is fluid and volatile, the new must necessarily flow from the old, the present from the past, the future from the present. In a remarkably effective analogy, he suggests that even the solid stone of "The Greek sculpture is all melted away, as if it had been statues of ice." Like Greek letters the statues are "tumbling into the inevitable pit which the creation of new thought opens for all that is old" (*CW*, II, 179–80). Nothing, in a word, is permanent.

Emerson's major concern here is the centrality of this absolute in Man's experience—namely, that there are no absolutes: "The life of man is a self-evolving circle . . . without end." Although "the inert effort of each thought" is to "heap itself," erect barricades, "if the soul is quick and strong, it bursts over that boundary on all sides, and expands another orbit." In short, "the heart refuses to be imprisoned" (*CW*, II, 180–81). The way in which Emerson sustains the circular image and metaphor as effectively and gracefully as he does is no less remarkable when we recognize that it is due as much to the care with which he chose so rich and evocative a symbol as to his conscious literary skill in handling it. The determinism or even fatalism one hears in the announcement that however "Sturdy and defying" the person may look, "he has a helm which he obeys" (*CW*, II, 180) becomes, if rightly understood, the springboard to an ever-renewing freedom which allows each of us to further realize his potential Self.

The next several paragraphs amplify the point that facts, thoughts, even laws are not ends but rather beginnings. "There is no outside, no enclosing wall, no circumference to us. . . . Men walk as prophecies of the next age" (*CW*, II, 181). Not even moods are frozen. The natural penchant to evolve is evident in our need to move past our fellows when we discover their limitations, to rise constantly through the successive plateaus of thought. Confronted by new versions of reality proposed by "Man Thinking"—the challenger of the conventional, the traditional, the status quo—no one and nothing is safe: science, literary reputation, fame, religion, manners, even morals. "Generalization is always a new influx of the divinity into the mind" (*CW*, II, 183). Each generation, each individual, enjoys the right and bears the responsibility to construct its own perceptions and understandings. Of course, such freedom demands substantial valor.

Emerson here shifts from culture to conversation for his illustrations and further asserts the centrality of the Self. "Conversation is a game of circles" (*CW*, II, 184); we move outward, onward, beyond the thoughts of successive speakers, and are ultimately left with the splendor of silence. We may fill our emptiness with the abundance of the literary heritage, for example, but must recognize that no mind, no work is final. So too with religion and the natural world: each of these is "a system of concentric circles" in which we observe the "law of eternal procession" (*CW*, II, 186). To drive home the point he draws on homely illustrations: "one man's beauty, another's ugliness; one man's wisdom, another's folly" and so forth (*CW*, II, 187).

Expecting the charge that moralists might level against him for seeming again to confuse vice with virtue, by making vice the predicate of virtue, he boldly announces that he is "not careful to justify" himself and, further, "that no evil is pure, nor hell itself without its extreme satisfactions" (*CW*, II, 188). Perhaps, as noted above, this is one of Emerson's most controversial positions, one which has probably nettled as many readers as any other logical extension or practical application of his Transcendentalism.

Again anticipating the Whitman of the 1855 "Preface" and the 1860 "Song of Myself," he announces: "I am only an experimenter. . . . I unsettle all things. No facts are to me sacred; none are profane; I simply experiment, an endless seeker, with no Past at my back" (*CW*, II, 188). The utterance shares the breathlessness and intensity of the transparent eye-ball passage in *Nature*. In a section which is key for understanding his vision, he admits that "this incessant movement and progression" which he is reporting are "sensible to us, [only] by contrast to some principle of fixture or stability in the soul" (*CW*, II, 188)—the Over-Soul, the Deity, God, "the still and silent center of the universe" envisioned by Augustine, Dante, and Eliot, among others.

In their controlled, prophetic quality, the concluding four paragraphs of the essay surpass the announcements of the orphic poet of the last chapter of *Nature*. Discarding if not condemning the "rags and relics" of the past, the "disease" of "old age," Emerson chants: "there is no sleep, no pause, no preservation, but all things renew, germinate, and spring." The natural metaphor is fitting and rich. "Infancy, youth, receptive, aspiring, with religious eye looking upward" shall embrace the "sacred" present and future, and "the past is always swallowed and forgotten." If there is any absolute it is that "Nothing is secure but life, transition, the energizing spirit. . . . Life is a series of surprises" (*CW*, II, 188–89). There is a pronounced note of Transcendental madness in the concluding paragraph of "Circles" as Emerson describes our "insatiable desire . . . to forget ourselves . . . to draw a new circle" and in so doing—here he uses the language of religious emotionalism—give ourselves to "enthusiasm" and soar to "abandonment." But he concludes the piece with a rhetorically compromising, though nevertheless pertinent, stricture: "Dreams and drunkenness, the use of opium and alcohol are the semblance and counterfeit of this oracular genius" (*CW*, II, 190).

Thematically, "Intellect" and "Art," the final essays in *Essays: First Series*, bring to a full circle the subjects to which Emerson addressed himself in the first two pieces in the book, "History" and "Self-Reliance." In both of these concluding essays he again considers the ultimate sources of man's insights and expressions and, almost predictably, discovers another occasion for insisting on the vitality of the present and future, as well as on the necessity for self-reliance.

In its insistent description of the growth and process inherent in genuine intellectual activity, "Intellect" grows from "Circles." Emerson pleads for spontaneity and states that ultimately "We have little control over our thoughts" but are "prisoners of ideas" (*CW*, II, 195). The truth which all people have the potential to receive cannot be corrected or contrived, or otherwise tampered with, for it will remain truth only in its pristine, spontaneously and intuitively received state. Most interesting and important, however—especially for those who might misunderstand Emerson's notion of spontaneity as an expression of licensed anarchy or period Romantic enthusiasm, or both—is his qualification that to produce great art the receiver must exercise "a certain control over the spontaneous states, without which no production is possible." Nature must be submitted to the "rhetoric of thought" (*CW*, II, 199).

The latter third of the essay concentrates on the integrity demanded of the truth-seeker. The way lies neither in excessive specialization nor in the young and inexperienced person's attempt to synthesize other people's perceptions. Rather, the intellect must be tuned to operate constantly. The scholar, as he had insisted several years earlier in the Phi Beta Kappa Address, must operate unfettered, using and discarding those influences of the past and present that touch him; in the end he must be intellectually self-reliant.

These notions of development and growth, ever-expanding process, are at the heart of these essays, just as they are central to Transcendental thought. They inform or supply a logical base for the entire collection and are crucial to the more important individual essays, "History," "Self-Reliance," "The Over-Soul," "Circles," and, as we have just seen, "Intellect." It is fitting, therefore, that Emerson should begin "Art," the last piece in the collection, with a condemnation of imitation and a plea for creativity. Just as "the soul is progressive," so each work of art it produces reaches toward a "new and fairer whole. . . . the artist must employ the symbols in use in his day and nation, to convey his enlarged sense to his fellow-men" (*CW*, II, 209–10). To this degree new art is formed from the old. Art denotes the high point of a given age, and those of any period who are touched by it have their encounter with the ultimate source, "an Aboriginal Power" (*CW*, II, 213).

But the Transcendentalist's principal aim is not to argue the universality of art. Rather he insists on the potential possessed by all people in every age. He concludes this short work by cautioning that the beautiful must not be divorced from the functional and by calling for the arts and artists "to find beauty and holiness in new and necessary facts" (*CW*, II, 218). As he had suggested in "The American Scholar" and would in "The Poet" (the lead essay in *Second Series*), the field, the roadside, railroad, insurance office—the innumerable commonplace realities we share in our culture—are worthy subjects precisely because they are nature and, therefore, sacred, holy, and moral.

Like the great majority of subjects he addresses in this first collection, the ideas Emerson explores are amplifications of themes he had sounded in *Nature* and his earlier prose, as well as poetry. This does not diminish the value of the essays but enhances it. They clarify his thought for us. Tightly constructed, occasionally pointed and even poetic, most of the essays are rich in rhetorical power and vigorous in their insights and assertions. Yet the arrangement is not lockstep; the coherence of the collection is not absolute. One reader may view the essays as dives into particular aspects of Emerson's Transcendental thought, deeper explorations of particular insights and propositions. Another reader, whose judgment is equally valid, might embrace the volume as circular in structure. Beginning and ending with challenges to imitation and demands for self-reliance, its middle explores the implications of these for Man and at the same time dwells on the principles which underlie and inform the changing landscape on which human life is unfolded.

Perhaps the difficulty and, from another point of view, the excitement of Emerson lies in his very hospitality to diversity, his willingness to explore, to leap, to entertain the range of possibilities. Portions of Emerson's journals have been described as "a running dialogue between his various selves." He was a "dramatist of ideas" who accepted and even celebrated the condition that we move from threshold to threshold.[16] The reader of Emerson, therefore, must appreciate the other than conventional modes of development which he employed in his prose. For example, the dialectical method of his thought might explain the rhetorical strategies of some essays and the organization of entire collections.[17] The never-ending quest, the eternal process, is suggested by the very thesis-antithesis-synthesis pattern, the process being repeated by the necessary transformation of each new synthesis into yet another thesis, which in turn serves as the predicate from which another stage of the process emanates.[18] This method of logic, whether polar, triadic, or hierarchical in its structure, is indeed a method—and it is logical, even though it is open-ended.[19] Its very organicism is, from one point of view, the special reason for Emerson's using the dialectical method. The essays in the first collection, for instance, might be paired according to polarities: "History" and "Self-Reliance," explorations of the Not Me and the Me; "Compensation" and "Spiritual Laws," considerations of the natural law of opposites and the principles which underlie it; and so forth.[20] Always willing to entertain possibilities, Emerson rides the pendulum from one end of its arc to the other. He was not merely throwing together his first two collections in "haphazard order," as was suggested of the second series by Rusk, his modern biographer.[21]

Emerson was a craftsman in control of his materials; he worked according to aesthetic principles, whether he was constructing a paragraph or sequence of paragraphs, composing an entire essay, or arranging a collection. He was no mere Romantic, as Romantics have been stereotyped, blurting out the discoveries of inspiration, but an artist.[22] Seeking an organic structure which would mirror, among other virtues, nature's wildness and oneness, [23] he not only discarded the conventions of ordinary exposition but adopted principles of rhetoric and style which are not always understood or observed by modern readers and authors. For example, eschewing clarity and reaching for suggestiveness—which is in keeping with the process of discovery—Emerson was less concerned with "static" elements such as structure than he was with "kinetic" elements, the organic development of images and ideas, for example. The written prose work was not so divorced from oral expression that it should not be influenced by the rhetorical strategies employed in preaching or even intelligent conversation, a favorite genre among the Transcendentalists, who assumed that art is a *process* of communication rather than a product.[24]

The death of his son Waldo in January 1842, and Emerson's apparent sense of diminishing energies and enthusiasms as he entered his forties are two of the many factors which contributed to the change in tone and philosophy between the two series of *Essays*. Of course, it is impossible for the biographer or intellectual historian to identify precisely the sequence of events in the intellectual or emotional life of any subject. Changes are rarely epiphanies; and, more important, epiphanies rarely occur in the life of a man as complex and subtle—as hospitable to the full range of possibilities—as Emerson. Nevertheless, it is evident that a fundamental transition in perspective and posture occurred in the few years between the publication of his two collections. By 1844 there has

been a muting—though not a disappearance—of the earlier revolutionary voice which had announced the powers and prerogatives of the
individual. The bold, vigorous assertions of Transcendental faith, the
visions of almost unbounded possibilities, give way, though not altogether, to a certain quietude, acquiescence, or even skepticism—
what has been described as a "renewed recognition of the dominion of
fate." [25] The Realities of his Transcendental Idealism do not disappear
after the early 1840s, but they are washed over by the waves of
experience. Emerson holds on to his faith but he does so in the face of a
growing sense of the "inherent absurdity"—or at least difficulty—"of
the human condition." [26] Again, while the drift is evident, the transition is neither abrupt nor complete. The earlier vision—which was not
without its bothersome sense of the powers which can determine life (as
we have seen in our discussion of "Compensation," for instance)—is not
discarded but, in keeping with Emerson's intellectual style, is modified
in response to the new facts of existence which experience has introduced. It is imperative, however, to understand that Fate implies a
beneficent tendency; although the individual might not be in absolute
control, he can make the best of a not altogether bad situation. And so
Emerson demonstrates a renewed interest in societal relations and a
willingness to explore the means by which one preserves his integrity
when under pressure from his contemporaries and civilized institutions. [27] In place of confrontation, even revolution, there is growing
evidence of deliberation. The most glaring exception to this new
Emersonian voice is the first piece in *Essays: Second Series,* "The Poet,"
which we shall consider at the beginning of the next chapter.

One of Emerson's most important essays, "Experience," offers a
provocative and dignified discussion of the middle-age Transcendentalist's reflections on life's testing of his faith. The essay is the
second in the collection of 1844, and in its muted, almost world-weary
tone, especially at its beginning, presents a persona quite different from
the celebrating optimist of the earlier work, including "The Poet,"
which precedes it. There is less certitude about life, although the
courage one heard in the prose of the past eight years is sustained.
"Illusion, Temperament, Succession, Surface, Surprise, Reality,
Subjectiveness,—these are threads on the loom of time, these are the
lords of life. . . . I know better than to claim any completeness for my
picture. I am a fragment, and this is a fragment of me" (*W,* III, 82–83).

If the title "Experience" suggests that Emerson is to present a concrete, empirical account of actuality, the reader's expectation soon collapses. In a passage which anticipates the autobiographical reflections and brooding tones of Eliot's *Four Quartets,* Emerson begins the essay by observing the dream-like, almost surreal dimensions of human experience. (The first-person plural pronoun he uses throughout moves in its suggestive references from the formal editorial to the wider embrace of shared human experience.) "Where do we find ourselves? In a series of which we do not know the extremes, and believe that it has none. We wake and find ourselves on a stair; there are stairs below us, which we seem to have ascended; there are stairs above us, many a one, which go upward and out of sight" (*W,* III, 45). The flow of experience is Platonic, Wordsworthian. The Genius who guards the threshold at which we enter life "gives us the lethe to drink" and we remain unable to "shake off the lethargy now at noonday. Sleep lingers all our lifetime about our eyes. . . . Ghostlike we glide through nature, and should not know our place again" (*W,* III, 45). The present is trivial, degraded, a prelude to the future toward which we always grope, and the past is equally unfulfilling. However, the dream-like flow of experience, the "opium . . . instilled into all disaster," has the virtue of soothing the pain of life. To illustrate the point that people unnecessarily "grieve and bemoan themselves" (*W,* III, 48), he recounts in a few sentences the psychological and spiritual struggle he had in reconciling himself to the death of his young son, Waldo.

The "evanescence and lubricity of all objects" is "the most unhandsome" aspect of the human condition, but is unavoidable. It is precisely that—a condition. "Dream delivers us to dream, and there is no end to illusion. Life is a train of moods like a string of beads" (*W,* III, 49–50). Flux, relativity, subjectivity are the rules of experience. But if there is a tone of lamentation in this initial recounting—Emerson's or what he is representing as the conventional perception of experience—the tone shifts to celebration. Being impossible, permanence is eschewed and the flux of experience, the transitory, are embraced. So what seems an unhappy condition which Man must learn to tolerate becomes the cornerstone in Emerson's attempt to construct a notion of what is.

In the next section of the essay he renews his attack on the excessively intellectual. "Life is not intellectual or critical, but sturdy" (*W,* III, 59), to be savored somewhere between sense and mind. The scholar, for

example, must strive to maintain a healthy balance between the two
elements that make up human life, "power and form" (*W,* III, 65).
Common sense and spontaneity are to be sought; excess and empirical
calculation are to be avoided. And, of course, various creeds are but
different versions of reality, individual perceptions. Subjectivity is the
condition: "Thus inevitably does the universe wear our color. . . . As I
am, so I see" (*W,* III, 79); however much society's institutions may hate
this truth, this subverter of authority, such is Man's condition.

The emphasis on the Self with which Emerson concludes "Experience" is maintained in the next essay in the collection, "Character." The
first fifteen paragraphs explore his rather evanescent description of
"character." But the latter portion of the piece considers the Self in
relation to society, the theme which dominates the rest of *Essays: Second
Series.* After pondering major historical figures, self-reliant people who
possess the crucial and essential quality, he concludes that it is like heat
and light, a natural, irresistible power. "Character," in a word, "is this
moral order" (*W,* III, 95), and he who possesses the trait becomes the
conscience of his society. These heroes resist circumstance. They force
events to follow them. They are unconventional, even uncivil and
unavailable, and because of their intensity and power they are wor-
shipped or hated by the societies they inhabit.

Emerson does not leave his self-sufficient person to confront the rest of
humanity. He attempts to define the proper relations his ideal people
might enjoy with their contemporaries. He knows of "nothing which
life has to offer so satisfying as the profound good understanding which
can subsist, after much exchange of good offices, between two virtuous
men" (*W,* III, 111), men of character, however infrequent the conjunc-
tion. What he is approaching here anticipates the deeply personal
observation Melville made to Hawthorne in a letter written at the time
of the publication of *Moby-Dick* when their relationship was most
intense: "But truth is ever incoherent, and when the big hearts strike
together, the concussion is a little stunning."[28]

Man's relationship to others and to his society is the major concern of
four of the remaining six essays in this second collection: "Manners,"
"Gifts," "Politics," and "New England Reformers"; only "Nature" and
"Nominalist and Realist" depart from this, the major theme of the
volume.

"Manners" is a restrained and mature discussion of the proper social relations to be maintained by the cultivated, self-reliant "gentleman" who possesses "character" and is a leader, a law-giver, "good company for pirates and good with academicians" (*W*, III, 125). Rightly comprehended and intelligently used, manners remove "avoidable obstructions" (*W*, III, 127) in our social intercourse; yet, unhappily enough, they soon become fixed, frozen in usage, and so are remnants of the Past and bedrocks of aristocracy. In discarding them, however, Emerson does not celebrate the sort of absolute democracy chanted by Whitman, for instance, nor does he envision an egalitarian society resulting from the sort of leveling warned of by Tocqueville.[29] Emerson is conservative. Challenging the antielitist thought of theoretical communists, as well as the leveling tendency of Jacksonian Democracy which so appalled Cooper and others not swept up by the enthusiasms of the 1830s and 1840s, Emerson asserts the "inevitable" selection process at work in any social organization: as a matter of course "a new class finds itself at the top, as certainly as cream rises in a bowl of milk: and if the people should destroy class after class, until two men only were left, one of these would be the leader and would be involuntarily served and copied by the other" (*W*, III, 129). All may have the potential even though only a handful realize it, but those leaders who appear do—indeed must—assert and enjoy their primacy, while those who for whatever causes must follow, will follow. Natural selection will have its way and the hero, the genuine gentleman, will flourish and lead.

"Nature," a short piece which follows "Gifts" (an avowed individualist's practical application of Transcendental principle to ordinary social transactions in modern commercial society), enhances the organization and thematic coherence of the entire volume and repeats his predominant concern for the individual in the social context. At the same time, this strategically placed essay ponders the more fundamental and fruitful relation which Man bears to nature and reinforces the central Transcendental themes of flux and growth.

From the relatively sublime, Emerson returns in the next essay to the eminently practical world of politics. With a vigor unexcelled by his other considerations of Man vis-à-vis the social and governmental mechanisms society has evolved, "Politics" offers a powerful defense of the individual against the encroachments of institutions. The challenge to institutional authority with which he opens the piece springs from the fundamental notion of flux, mutability. The premises he establishes are harbingers of the sort of skepticism at the heart of Thoreau's political writings. Asserting that a societal institution, like a law, is merely a single "man's expedient to meet a particular case," he insists that any seemingly "aboriginal" body might be altered. He disabuses youth of the illusion that any form is anything but "a rope of sand which perishes in the twisting" and puts his trust in the "old statesman" who "knows that society is fluid" (W, III, 199–200).

Driving to the heart of classical and modern legal thinking, he initiates an extended discussion of the two basic objects for which government exists: to protect persons and property. Measured by modern liberal standards, Emerson's political position is conservative. People may possess equal rights in general, but their claims on property are as unequal as their respective possession of character. Acknowledging the period's concern about the inheritance of property, he rejects the remedies proposed by reformers, especially the "young and foolish" (W, III, 204). He labels each age's youthful majority "ignorant and deceivable" and warns that were they able to effect their reforms, "States would soon run to ruin." The consolation, however, is that "things refuse to be trifled with. Property will be protected" (W, III, 204–205). In some socialist utopia—the American 1830s and 1840s spawned and hosted a multitude of such schemes—the law may deny even the power of the vote to the property owner; "Nevertheless, by a higher law, the property will, year after year, write every statute that respects property" (W, III, 206). Of course, the financial cushion provided by his inheritance from Ellen Tucker, his first wife, and by his second wife's dowry enabled Emerson to conduct his life rather comfortably as an independent lecturer and author.

Emerson next turns his attention to the cultural and political arrogance which impels his contemporary Americans to so enthusiastically attempt to export political institutions. If Emerson appears conservative, even reactionary, in his views on property, his tolerance qualifies him as a liberal in extremis by any period's standards—a point not to be taken lightly. He is categorically opposed to any person or group imposing its will on another. Modes of government, he asserts, may not be grafted upon any society but must grow organically according to the culture's needs. Even monarchy is defended against unreflective and simplistic assaults by zealots of modern democracy.

Emerson is essentially skeptical and even cynical about the State. Anticipating the iconoclasm of Thoreau by at least five years, he announces that "Every actual State is corrupt. Good men must not obey the laws too well." Born of "benign necessity" yet inevitably condemned to "practical abuse" (*W*, III, 208), governments, like parties, pose threats to the precious freedom of the individual. Even the handful of parties founded on and dedicated to principle "degenerate into personalities, or would inspire enthusiasm" (*W*, III, 209), in the worst theological connotation of the word. And he proceeds to define the inherent liabilities of both conservative and radical thought and behavior in a more practical, applied fashion than he had even in the earlier lectures. Since "The spirit of our American radicalism is destructive and aimless. . . . not loving," and conservatism is "timid, and merely defensive of property," Mankind cannot expect to benefit from their influence in "science, art, or humanity" to any degree "commensurate with the resources of the nation" (*W*, III, 210). Despite this biting analysis of defects he does not "despair of our republic." Forced to choose he would prefer America's brawling, inefficient, and even corrupt governmental institutions. With enthusiasm he paraphrases the nautical metaphor of the early Federalist statesman Fisher Ames: "a monarchy is a merchantman, which sails well, but will sometimes strike on a rock and go to the bottom; whilst a republic is a raft, which would never sink, but then your feet are always in water." At this point he plants his optimist firmly in the soil of determinism and invokes his reader to "trust infinitely to the beneficent necessity which shines through all laws" (*W*, III, 211–12).

Again anticipating the social and political radicalism of Thoreau, he concludes "Politics" by turning his attention to the centrality and sanctity of the individual. Condemning encroachments on anyone's liberty, his solution echoes Jefferson: "Hence the less government we have the better,—the fewer laws, and the less confided power"(*W*, III, 215). To counter the abuses of government we have private character, which ultimately will negate the need for the state. The realistically colored vision he offers at the end of the essay promises individual self-government in a world which has developed to a point where it eschews force while it recognizes the value of public institutions and services.

"Politics" is a moving and candid assessment of political realities as Emerson saw them. Grounded in a skepticism and caution about human nature which he would not allow in most other contexts—such as the theological debate over Calvinism's tenet regarding natural depravity—the essay should dispel any conceptions of Emerson the Transcendentalist groping in the fogs of his own abstractions. It reveals an astute and cautious political observer, a man capable of translating the essential principles of his Transcendental faith into practical political terms. The individual's freedom is always paramount for Emerson. If it is necessary to classify his political thinking, it is probably most accurate to recognize that many of his ideas stem from the agrarian tradition, the heritage of Jefferson and, despite his reservations, Jackson. Emerson's individualism, as well as his faith in laissez-faire capitalist economics, though, testify to his intellectual and spiritual values rather than his allegiance to particular parties, interest groups, or systems. Distrustful of the masses, particularly of the people's judgment, he was a supporter of the natural aristocracy, a man whose roots and predilections lay in the conservative Federalist-Whig tradition; practical politics were always problematical for him.[30]

In "Nominalist and Realist" Emerson stands back philosophically and, as he had in the essay on "Nature" in this collection, achieves some degree of distance from the matters he has been confronting. He begins by pondering the human limitations he recognizes in himself and others. But by the end of the essay, as a result of perceiving them in light of the immutable laws of flux and subjectivism which he has been emphasizing in this book, he is able not only to reconcile the difficulties, but even to celebrate the diversity they insure.

First, he complains of the difficulty one has pinpointing ideas in people. Individuals, even great people, are the victims of gifts and talents which fixate them as well as distort them in the eyes of others. Each person, even Jesus, would in fact be a tyrant, bending others to his version of reality. Emerson drives home the rationale for diversity in homely fashion: "Since we are all so stupid, what benefit that there should be two stupidities!" And in a biting aphoristic style he collapses the modern tendency to centralize and to attempt "the consolidation of all men into a few men. If John was perfect, why are you and I alive?" (*W*, III, 239–40). This is perhaps the ultimate empirical observation upon which he has constructed his faith in the individual, the center of his Transcendental optimism: "For rightly every man is a channel through which heaven floweth" (*W*, III, 242).

As he nears the end of this speculation, which has become a vigorous assertion, he offers a well-wrought, even polished, condensation of the practical effects of flux, growth, subjectivism, and the potential for reconciliation which resides in nature and Man. He concludes by using his own penchant for change, his hospitality to contradictory perceptions; *nothing,* including Emerson himself, is set in stone: "I am always insincere, as always knowing there are other moods," a man who likes "everything by turns and nothing long" (*W,* III, 247–48).

In "New England Reformers" he continues his assault on those who would tyrannize others by insisting on their own truth. These are the distorters who are fixated on the social or political ill which they have identified and which they have dedicated themselves to remedying. There is genuine humor in the beginning of the essay where Emerson offers an almost comic retrospective of the American reform movement, especially in his native region, which burgeoned for almost half a century before the Civil War. He wryly observes that "In these movements nothing was more remarkable than the discontent they begot in the movers." Those concerned with various religious reforms "defied each other, like a congress of kings." The spirit spread to virtually all segments of society, to the point that "Even the insect world was to be defended [which, of course, spawned] a society for the protection of ground-worms, slugs and mosquitos" (*W,* III, 251–53). These were complemented by the fads of homeopathy, hydropathy, mesmerism, and phrenology. What he is cataloguing is an abundance of social-change groups run amok, one of the more significant characteristics of American society in the 1840s. There is virtually no institution which does not undergo the keenest scrutiny. Emerson recognizes the advantages of all this radical din: "a tendency to the adoption of simpler methods" in order to free the citizenry from the burdens and snares of too much organization, and also "an assertion of the sufficiency of the private man." But he can only register chagrin, laced again with a wry comic sense, as he characterizes the disadvantages of such well-intentioned, nevertheless myopic, activity: "the threatened individual immediately excommunicated the church, in a public and formal process" (*W,* III, 254). He welcomes the new spirit of individual assertion but is repelled by the reformers' offensiveness. "They are partial; they are not equal to the work they pretend. They lose their way. . . . and lose their sanity and power of benefit" (*W,* I, 261). He concludes that it is better to remain in the establishment and be superior to it than to delude oneself by thinking that the correction of one evil will regenerate the whole.

Not only does he challenge the reformers' fragmented and partial views, and the inevitable distortions in their criticism and remedy, he questions whether their organizations can be able and good except at the beginning. The bandwagons once built lumber mindlessly through the worlds of politics, education, and other institutions. Very clearly he is offering an explanation of his own refusal to participate in Ripley's Brook Farm experiment, for example, or to lend anything more than moral support to other attempts at reform, at least at this point in his career. These views and attitudes are perfectly in keeping with other practical applications of Transcendental principles in the political and economic spheres. The detachment and caution—skepticism, if you will—which pervade an essay such as "Politics" inform his opinions on reform. It is the same detachment and caution he sounded in "History," the lead essay in the first collection. Just as an excessive reverence for the past threatens individual autonomy, so do peer pressure, enthusiasm— in the worst sense of the word—and bandwagons generally.[31] As deep as his sympathies with the idea of reform may have been, he kept his distance and, except on the issue of slavery, became progressively disillusioned about it.

In the latter half of "New England Reformers" he offers an almost lyrical celebration of the individual; Man is the more worthy, the only, object of regeneration. And so he concludes the cycle of exploration he had initiated with the first two pieces of *Essays: First Series,* three years earlier. "Friendship and association are very fine things, and a grand phalanx of the best of the human race, banded for some catholic object; yes, excellent; but remember that no society can ever be so large as one man" (*W,* III, 264–65). Union must ultimately be inward and no person's development may be cramped by association with others, by connections which inevitably impede personal development. Challenging the cynicism and skepticism which inform institutions such as education, as well as the despair which undermines faith in the individual, he insists that "The soul lets no man go without some visitations and holydays of a diviner presence" (*W,* III, 271). He vigorously condemns Calvinistic notions of Man's depravity and concludes that "as a man is equal to the Church and equal to the State, so he is equal to every other man" (*W,* III, 280).

With the publication of *Essays: Second Series* in 1844, the forty-one-year-old Emerson completed a cycle of statements in prose which provides the principal support for his reputation as a major American thinker and author. This is not to suggest that after the mid-1840s he wrote no prose of importance or enduring value. But the eight years following the publication of *Nature* form his most creative, most provocative and most engaging period. There would be other statements, particularly in the 1850s, which would endure, and there is the poetry he had been composing since he was a schoolboy and would continue to write until old age prevented him. These achievements, however, would never eclipse the brilliance of this early prose.

Chapter Four
Artful Thunder

Emerson was forty-three years old when the first of his three volumes of poetry was issued on Christmas Day 1846. (It bears the publication date 1847.) Before any reader addresses himself to the verse, however, it is helpful to have some understanding of Emerson's theory of poetry and his views about the poet's purposes and functions. Properly understood, the poet and his art are central in the Transcendental fabric Emerson wove.

His interest in the subject began early—when he was a schoolboy, in fact—and grew with the years. He read widely and analytically, and was sensitive, discriminating, and articulate on the subject, as is evident from the great amount of space he devoted to aesthetic theory, poets, and poetry in his journals, letters, and lectures. In addition to these numerous references during the 1830s and early 1840s, as well as later, he offered one entire presentation, "The Poet," in the lecture series on "The Times" which he gave in 1841–42. But he made his most comprehensive and lasting utterance on the matter in the opening piece in *Essays: Second Series* (1844), also titled "The Poet." Here he presented the major portion of his mature thought on the role of the poet, as well as his theory of poetry.

In the essay Emerson states that the poet shares the Universe with two other children, the "Knower" and the "Doer," lovers of truth and goodness, respectively. The triumvirate is completed by the poet, the lover of beauty, the "Sayer," or "Namer." Emerson repeats the essential proposition of the Transcendental movement, that nature is symbolic, the universe emblematic; at the same time he reiterates the limitations of the Understanding, the path followed by the sensual man such as the scientist. And he concludes that although "The people fancy they hate poetry," they are, in fact, "all poets and mystics!" (*W*, III, 16–17).

This true poet, this arch-Transcendentalist, however, is discovered only infrequently. Not a mere "thinker," a "man of talent," he is "Man

Thinking." His is the genius which will eradicate the ugly as he reintegrates those things which are dislocated and detached from God by perceiving their essential unity with nature and the Whole; the poet grasps the spiritual significance even of the factory-village, the railroad, and, of course, what is ordinarily comprehended as the natural world. By means of his superior insight the poet can induce a sort of transcendence, leading his reader to a vision similar to that described in the transparent eye-ball passage in *Nature,* among other places. Emerson confides that he himself experiences this kind of soaring when he reads a poem which he trusts as an inspiration: "And now my chains are to be broken; I shall mount above these clouds and opaque airs in which I live . . . and from the heaven of truth I shall see and comprehend my relations . . . . This day shall be better than my birthday: then I became an animal; now I am invited into the science of the real" (*W,* III, 12). In guiding us through nature, through experience, the poet "unlocks our chains and admits us to a new scene," leads us across the chasm to life and truth, and rescues us from the ironic fate of the "poor shepherd, who, blinded and lost in the snow-storm, perishes in a drift within a few feet of his cottage door" (*W,* III, 33). The ultimate, successful Transcendentalist, "the poet turns the world to glass, and shows us all things in their right series and procession" (*W,* III, 20). Poets are "liberating gods" (*W,* III, 32). Capable of that which all would rightly desire, they stand "among partial men for the complete man. . . . the man without impediment, who . . . traverses the whole scale of experience, and is representative of man, in virtue of being the largest power to receive and to impart." Representing beauty, the poet "is a sovereign, and stands on the centre" (*W,* III, 5–7). He is not merely an arranger, a compiler or composer of meters but a "diviner," a "prophetic speaker," whether in verse or prose, in the vatic tradition. For his conception Emerson was actually reaching back to the ancient notion of the bard, echoing conventional Romantic notions of the poet.[1]

Emerson's poetic theory is intimately related to this conception of the poet. Perhaps the clearest and most widely known public statement he made on the theory of poetry was in the eighth paragraph of the essay "The Poet" where he announced that "it is not metres, but a metre-making argument that makes a poem,—a thought so passionate and alive that . . . it has an architecture of its own, and adorns nature with a new thing. The thought and the form are equal in the order of time, but in the order of genesis the thought is prior to the form" (*W,* III, 9–10). This precept that form is secondary probably helped inspire Whitman, for example, to be hospitable to the freedoms and new disciplines of *vers libre.* But the reader of Emerson's own poetry must be taken aback by his generally close adherence to his period's formal requirements, its conventions of verse. With few exceptions his poems scan easily and offer discernible rhyme schemes and regular line lengths.

His views on the technical requirements of verse are germane. In "Poetry and Imagination"—published in 1875, though portions were composed as early as the 1840s (*W,* VIII, 357–58)—for example, where he considers matters such as rhyme and meter, it is evident that he was in command of his materials and willing to insist on the conventions of English prosody because he understood their value, not because he accepted them blindly. He defends "the charm of rhyme to the ear" (*W,* VIII, 45) for the relief it offers from monotony and for the symmetry its very repetition provides. He also argues that the poet should allow poetry to "pass . . . into music and rhyme. . . . [which] is the transparent frame that allows almost the pure architecture of thought to become visible to the mental eye. Substance is much, but so are mode and form much" (*W,* VIII, 52–53). In a similar fashion he insists on the naturalness of meter by suggesting that "Metre begins with pulse-beat, and the length of lines in songs and poems is determined by the inhalation and exhalation of the lungs. If you hum or whistle the rhythm of the common English metres . . . you can easily believe these metres to be organic, derived from the human pulse, and to be therefore not proper to one nation, but to mankind" (*W,* VIII, 46). Since Emerson understood the conventions he observed in his own verse to be "organic," it seems unfair to criticize him for not realizing in his own poetry the innovations Whitman achieved.

My purpose in this chapter is to discuss most of those poems which seem likely in my judgment to endure in the canon of American poetry. Certainly, not all are great. Many are of middling quality, some are uneven, and a few merely possess eminently quotable lines. What they do collectively, however, is demonstrate a more than respectable achievement in poetry by one of America's principal literary men.

To facilitate matters, particularly for those who are coming to Emerson's poetry for the first time, the poems are discussed within thematic groupings, the most important of which are the role of the poet, Man's relationship to nature, the public issues such as slavery which led to the Civil War, and personal subjects such as love and death. Although this arrangement seems preferable to a discussion of the development of Emerson's poetry in chronological order, my attempt to offer a coherent framework for sensible discussion should not—indeed, must not—preclude a reader's approaching any poem by a different avenue. My framework is a matter of convenience, not an attempt to fix Emerson's rich work in a set of categories.

"Merlin," one of the finest poems in the first collection, reveals Emerson's conception of the poet and his role, and also illustrates his reliance on the "renaissance tradition of paradox."[2] The speaker opens "Merlin I" with a tight assertion of what is and is not the "artful thunder" of bardic poetry: "Its chords should ring as blows the breeze, / Free, peremptory, clear" in order to "make the wild blood start / In its mystic springs." Having told us in no uncertain terms in the first eight lines that form and style, however pleasing, do not constitute the poem, he proceeds to describe the poet and his verse. Not merely a skilled and pleasing musician—a man of talent—this speaker's "kingly bard," Merlin, "Must smite the chords rudely and hard" in order to render organic poetry, the

> Artful thunder, which conveys
> Secrets of the solar track,
> Sparks of the supersolar blaze.
> (*W,* IX, 120)

This bard, unencumbered "With the coil of rhythm and number," shall in his transcendence " 'mount to paradise / By the stairway of surprise' " (*W,* IX, 121). Anticipating the theme of opposites to be explored at the start of "Merlin II," Emerson further defines the centrality of paradox to the workings of the bard. Beguiled by Sybarites—the wild dancers of the rituals of classical mythology—Merlin with his "mighty line / Extremes of nature reconciled" (*W,* IX, 122).

The second poem commences by amplifying this pairing, the balancing and compensating Emerson dwells upon in both series of *Essays:*

"Balance-loving Nature / Made all things in pairs" (*W,* IX, 123). It is little wonder that Emerson should dismiss the verse of those he judged to be merely talented,[3] jingle-men such as Poe. What he sought, as he stated it succinctly in "Poetry and Imagination," was "The original force, the direct smell of the earth or the sea" as he found them in ancient poetry: the Sagas, English and Scottish balladry, bardic poetry, and, to the point, "Gawain's parley with Merlin" in *Morte d'Arthur,* which he quotes at length (*W,* VIII, 57–63).

He concludes "Merlin II" with an oblique yet incisive description of the price, the "ruin rife," the poet must pay for the genuine bardic experience—the paradox of Merlin, "music-drunken," surrendering his liberty and control to the Fates in order to achieve a more organic relationship with the universe and, therefore, the insight to prophecy. When we consider this paradox, we should recognize the happy balance Emerson strikes in the form of "Merlin." He comes quite close to his own ideal of "metre-making argument" by achieving a successful mixture of the accepted conventions of nineteenth-century verse: the Common Meter of the initial four lines of "Merlin I" and the traditional rhyme schemes and regular line lengths of most of both poems are set off opposite the skillful "irregularly rhymed 'free verse'" of the second stanza of "Merlin I."[4]

Another of his most successful efforts to explore the poet and his art is "Bacchus" (1847). The speaker here seeks the same "wildest freedom" and ecstatic abandon suggested in the "Merlin" poems. Indeed, striving to cast off the restraints of the Understanding, mere common-sense perceptions of experience, the poet courts transcendence, a merging of his Self with creation "Which on the first day drew . . . The dancing Pleiads and eternal men" (*W,* IX, 127). The importance of this god to Emerson's thinking is perhaps suggested by his reference more than a quarter-century later when he discussed transcendence near the end of "Poetry and Imagination": "O celestial Bacchus! drive them mad,— this multitude of vagabonds, hungry for eloquence, hungry for poetry, starving for symbols, perishing for want of electricity" (*W,* VIII, 70). In the transcendent experience described in "Bacchus" and elsewhere there is a suggestion of what has been termed the "inverted mysticism" of Whitman's poetry: the achievement of merger and vision not through asceticism but by means of bathing in sensual experience.[5] This aspect of Emerson is beautifully articulated in the colloquial and pithy "Berrying" (1847), one of his better short poems, in which he uses Calvinist theology to assert the hedonism of the speaker. The irony of the speaker's discovering "dreams thus beautiful" and "wisdom" in the "Ethiops sweet" drives home with singular force his rejection of his Puritan forebears' conception of earth as "a howling wilderness" (*W*, IX, 41).[6]

But the exhilaration, or even ecstasy, enjoyed by the genuine poet requires that he suffer detachment from other men. "Saadi" (1842), Emerson's tribute to the Persian author he so admired, is one of his clearest poetic expressions of the loneliness and promise of the poet. Writing for the most part in octosyllabic couplets, Emerson commences the poem in rather breathless, short lines and immediately justifies the bard's aloofness by tracing it back to God's charge that the poet " 'Sit aloof.' " Saadi, who "dwells alone" (*W*, IX, 130), nevertheless loves Mankind. With the integrity of the scholar Emerson had described in his Phi Beta Kappa address, the poet ignores the din of life, reads his runes rightly, minds only his rhyme and listens solely to the whisper of the Muse: "Heed not what the brawlers say, / Heed thou only Saadi's lay" (*W*, IX, 133). Detachment and commitment are, of course, prerequisites for the conventional Romantic sort of insight and inspiration, but they assure that the poet's words will reveal "Terror and beauty" as well as "Nature veritable" (*W*, IX, 134). The upshot, the Muse promises, will be the opening of "innumerable doors" from which truth and goodness will flow, and so the poet will be admitted to the "perfect Mind" (*W*, IX, 135). The promise and the poem conclude with a suggestion that the ultimates sought by the poet reside in the commonplace, the "crones," "gossips," "drones" who "rise in stature / To the height of mighty Nature" to reveal the secret "Fraudulent Time in vain concealed": "That blessed gods in servile masks / Plied for thee thy household tasks" (*W*, IX, 135). If "Saadi" is not one of Emerson's more memorable poetic statements, it is one of his more forthright expressions on the subject, purpose, and means available to the poet.

The enchanting silent word picture of the "hypocritic Days," the "Daughters of Time," offered in the first six lines of "Days" (1857) is in fact a pantomime, a virtually soundless rehearsal of ritual. But in this complex work, Emerson questions his own adequacy to realize the role of the poet. Richly visual, the only noises are the "Muffled" marching steps of the "barefoot dervishes," the Mohammedan friars of the simile.

The statement which follows in this superb performance in blank verse
is equally low key and direct. Emerson simply admits the dissolving, if
not unwitting betrayal, of his "morning wishes" to penetrate or transcend; and in the last two lines he reports the "scorn" for his failure by
the now personified Day. What he manages to offer here is a thoroughly
uncluttered and restrained lament about his own inability to soar above
the barricades and tangles of the "pleached garden" (*W*, IX, 228) of his
life. (The poem was composed in 1851.) The muted pain and abiding
dignity the reader senses, and should respond to sympathetically, arise
from the speaker's own recognition of his dilemma, even though he is
unable to promise to resolve it.[7]

We experience the same sort of quiet, dignified acceptance of the
limitations of Man in "Brahma." Also published first in 1857, it is one
of the works in which Emerson most clearly finds his method in the
tradition of paradoxy and, thematically, conjures up a vision and truth
virtually unrelated to earlier, more hopeful, poems. The utterances of
the speaker—Brahma, the divine reality of post-Vedic mythology—in
this conventional sixteen-line poem are controlled, almost matter-of-
fact. From the first stanza the voice emphasizes its mystery and Man's
inability to fathom it:

> If the red slayer think he slays,
>   Or if the slain think he is slain,
> They know not well the subtle ways
>   I keep, and pass, and turn again.
> (*W*, IX, 195)

In the second stanza its secrets become even more impenetrable when it
announces the superiority of its comprehension in contrast to Man's: "Far
or forgot to me is near" and "The vanished gods to me appear." The
voice emphasizes the central paradox of existence—"Shadow and sun-
light," "shame and fame"—which is as indistinguishable as the conditions of the slayer and slain of the first stanza. In stanza 3 the Brahma
moves to yet another level of mystery by collapsing the logical distinctions ordinarily made between agent and act, or means: flyer and wings,
doubter and doubt, singer and song. The final quatrain deepens the
confusion, first by asserting the inevitable frustration of those who seek
him—who yearn to master his "subtle ways"—and then by holding

forth the possibility of success—"But thou, meek lover of the good! / Find me." The result, however, will raise the ultimate paradox for the speaker; discovering the answer, "turn thy back on heaven." More than implying mere resignation about Man's incapacity to comprehend, the statement here might induce moral and intellectual paralysis or suspension. It might even be read as profoundly autobiographical, a late statement of Emerson's detachment from contemporary events which has bothered so many critics. On the other hand, more enthusiastic readers who place him in the Renaissance tradition of paradoxy might view the work as his "strongest expression of his religious intuitions"[8] and of his genuine liberality.

It is clear that the Transcendental experience in its widest definition is the subject of most of Emerson's poetry. Some of his best recounts the substance of the poet's nonrational encounter with the "Not-Me," as he phrased the world beyond Self in *Nature,* and others explore the dangers and pain of the role itself. Many more, also successful and enduring, focus on nature, including Man's connections to it. Some celebrate Man's right relation to nature while others criticize the materialism of modern culture which distorts life by precluding our having healthy links to the natural world. Two of the more enduring among the earlier nature poems are "Each and All" (1839) and "The Snow-Storm" (1841).

Judged to be Emerson's "first unquestionably great poem,"[9] "The Snow-Storm" was written during the winter of 1834–35. The first of its two stanzas of blank verse offers a general description of the arriving snow as it "veils the farm-house at the garden's end"; notes a foundered sled and the traveler it carries; and, finally, locates the speaker and the reader in the cozy warmth of a classic country homestead inhabited by people seated about "the radiant fireplace, enclosed / In a tumultuous privacy of storm" (*W,* IX, 41–42). What Emerson presents here is the conventional setting for the traditional event celebrated in so much New England poetry, the snow-storm. The nineteen lines which comprise the second stanza are among the most vivid and artistically wrought performances in poetic imagery in Emerson's canon. The artist of the passage, the north wind, "Curves his white bastions with projected roof / Round every windward stake, or tree, or door." Then "Mockingly, / On coop or kennel he hangs Parian wreaths; / A swan-like form invests the hidden thorn" (*W,* IX, 42). The familiar world is enhanced and mystified not randomly or by chance but consciously by art; with dazzling simplicity

Emerson conjures up the classic and gleaming white statuary of ancient
Greece by referring to the famed marbles of the island of Paros, which is
similar to the snowed-in farm not only in its statues but in its pristine
artifacts. The stormy, wild, creative period finished, the northwind

> Leaves, when the sun appears, astonished Art
> To mimic in slow structures, stone by stone,
> Built in an age, the mad wind's night-work,
> The frolic architecture of the snow.
> (*W*, IX, 42)

As the poem challenges materialism it celebrates the nourishment provided Man by sympathetic communion with nature.[10]

"Each and All," another of the poems composed in 1834—the year
which probably was a turning-point in Emerson's poetic development—
is another of the finest products of his early career. Composed of only
fifty-one lines, it signals a major advance in his perception of Man's
relation to nature; by using Reason rather than Understanding the poet
perceives unity amid the diversity of the world. Emerson has moved
beyond the awe which the natural world inspired among contemporaries
who merely observed and classified, and has come to sense a profound if
unspoken resonance in nature.[11]

The poem is traditional and conventional in its meters, its logical
tripartite structure, and its virtually unrelieved rhymed, occasionally
closed, couplets; only three lines are without mates and only the eight
lines which commence the final section slip into an *ababcded* pattern.
Emerson wisely balances the formality of the technique, however, with
the commonplace and simple—but nevertheless evocative—inhab-
itants of nature. Following his observation that "All are needed by each
one; / Nothing is fair or good alone" (*W*, IX, 4)—a principle which
emerges from his observation that nature's creatures, including Man,
indeed affect each other—he proceeds to test the proposition by noting
the discordance, even the ugliness, of the sparrow, the seashell, and the
bride when they are wrenched from their natural settings. This is one
facet of the truth he covets in line 37, the beginning of the third and
final part of the poem; penetrating the wood more deeply—
encountering on a sensual level the ground-pine, club-moss burrs,
violets, oaks, and acorns, as well as the sky, the river, and the morning

bird—he reports that "Beauty through my senses stole; / I yielded myself to the perfect whole" (*W*, IX, 6). In this celebratory and rising couplet we hear a suggestion of the same sort of Transcendental sympathy, even merging, he was to detail so often. If the psychological and spiritual significances and nuances are not uttered here, as they so frequently are in his later writings, it is probably because the experience is novel. But, of course, Emerson was never able or even desirous to reduce the Transcendental experience to the terms of the Understanding; such an attempt, even if conceivable, would necessarily have been frustrated. This reluctance is central in his poetry and should be borne in mind. Emerson frequently prefers to suggest rather than state.

Another of his more successful expressions of Man's proper relationship to nature is "The Rhodora." Composed of two eight-line parts, each with an *aabbcdcd* rhyme scheme, it possesses the formal structure of a seventeenth-century meditation. But Emerson chose a binary—question-and-answer—form, rather than the conventional triadic structure employed by the Metaphysicals. What he omits is the analytical portion of traditional structure and so almost casually dismisses the Understanding; the point is driven home by his memorable couplet, "Tell them, dear, that if eyes were made for seeing, / Then Beauty is its own excuse for being" (*W*, IX, 38). The ironic and knowing "simple ignorance" of the penultimate line of the poem signals that he is soaring above matters such as classification (Understanding) to the insight, the vision, born of Reason, that "The self-same Power that brought me there brought you" (*W*, IX, 38).[12]

Having come this far in our consideration of Emerson's nature poetry, let us turn for a moment to his occasionally scathing criticism of those who maintain a corrupt, even perverted relationship with the natural world.

Emerson is not deluded as are the sturdy, practical, sensual landlords of "Hamatreya" (1847). These men, including Bulkeley, one of Emerson's own ancestors, having owned and cultivated the land according to their own limited, earthbound purposes, lie in the ground; meanwhile, the "Earth laughs in flowers, to see her boastful boys / Earth-proud, proud of the earth which is not theirs" (*W*, IX, 35)—the boastful boys being their successors who live at a similar level of Understanding. Near the conclusion of the first two stanzas, which are composed in virtually unrelieved blank verse, the poet offers his ironic prediction of the inevitable results of their delusions: "Ah! the hot owner sees not Death, who adds / Him to his land, a lump of mould the more" (*W,* IX, 36). The speaker in the poem comprehends the myopia, the fatuousness and vanity of the Understanding, but arrogance or ignorance prevents these boastful boys from recognizing their own foolishness and tragedy. As an ironic condemnation of the causes and limitations of sensuality and materialism, "Hamatreya" is one of Emerson's most successful poems.

The deficiencies of these landlords are counterpointed by the second portion of the poem, "Earth-Song." The irony and paradox of its message is echoed in its compressed, runic lines; the climax occurs in the representative fourth stanza when the Earth observes that all who would have owned the land are gone and asks,

> ["]How am I theirs,
> If they cannot hold me,
> But I hold them?"
> (*W,* IX, 37)

And in case the reader has failed to comprehend the message, the poet concludes the poem with a quatrain whose form is closer to that of the bardic cadence of the "Earth-Song" than it is to the more traditional blank verse of the first two stanzas:[13]

> When I heard the Earth-song
> I was no longer brave;
> My avarice cooled
> Like lust in the chill of the grave.
> (*W,* IX, 37)

"Guy" (1847) is another of Emerson's poems which explore Man's wrong relations to nature. Guy is one of the company of Bulkeley, Hunt, Willard, and the rest in "Hamatreya." Working on so low a level with nature, Guy the materialist is clearly the dupe, thoroughly deserving of being "guyed" and made the butt of Emerson's and our ridicule.[14] He is perhaps representative of those smooth mediocrities who were and are bent on exploiting the earth for as much as they can get out of it.

One of Emerson's most forthright poetic statements about the modern perversion of nature is "Blight" (1844). The voice of the speaker is vigorous, assertive, nearly angry. It commences with an intense demand born of weariness: "Give me truths." The speaker is "weary of the surfaces" and "die[s] of inanition" (*W*, IX, 139). There follows a no less sharp or less ambiguous expression of impatience with those who are content with superficial, even false, relations with nature, "these young scholars, who invade our hills" but "Love not the flower they pluck, and know it not." When they engage nature these classifying botanists receive and give little but "Latin names" (*W*, IX, 140). Unlike the men of an earlier age who were more in touch with reality and "studied magic in the flowers, / And human fortunes in astronomy"—those "unitarians of the united world" who "wheresoever their clear eye-beams fell, / They caught the footsteps of the SAME" (*W*, IX, 140)—we of the modern world do not love the elements but are "thieves / And pirates of the universe" (*W*, IX, 141) who infect the natural world with the blight of our souls. Utterly divorced from nature, Man is a stranger to the stars, the mystic beast and bird, the plant and the vine. The result is that the elements "haughtily return us stare for stare" (*W*, IX, 140), one of Emerson's most forceful lines.

A somewhat less successful poem is "The World-Soul" (1847), in which Emerson counterpoises the civilized and the natural in lucid fashion and expresses his vibrant Transcendental optimism. After commencing in stanza 1 with a chant of thanksgiving for nature and humanity, he offers one of his most unequivocal denunciations of the hallmarks of modern technological and urban civilization. He condemns our vice and folly, base politics, uninspiring literature, and our commerce—in short, the corrupt or fallen state of Man and society. But the poem is principally an affirmation of the hope and promise which lie at the heart of creation, despite Man's inability to fathom them. Destiny, the "patient Daemon" (*W*, IX, 18), we are told, will prevail; and the speaker prophesies that in the course of the world's development, "He will from wrecks and sediment / The fairer world complete." Further, "He forbids to despair . . . And the unimagined good of men / Is yeaning at the birth" (*W*, IX, 19). The last stanza's rich imagery suggests youth, spring, love, summer, and warmth.

One issue which every serious reader must at some time confront is the degree to which Emerson's pastoralism turned him against the

developments of urban industrialism in nineteenth-century America.
Of course, his dilemma has been shared by intellectuals and artists,
including serious writers, since the advent of the industrial revolution.
Emerson, as we have seen, has generally been viewed as a figure in the
agrarian tradition.[15] His Romantic bias, with its implicit rejection of
materialism, has been interpreted as an attempt by him and his fellow
Transcendentalists to recapture a sense of awe in the face of nature, a
sense of wonder which materialistic urban industrialism had stolen
from them.[16] The question can also be explored from a different stance
that questions this judgment that Emerson was categorically hostile to
the city, an arch-symbol of life in the nineteenth century. The suggestion is that Emerson's observation of the dichotomy between the city
and nature was not a conclusion but a point of departure for his hope
that the city would become more organically related to nature. His hero
was neither bumpkin nor slicker, but the reconciler of the pastoral and
urban, the cosmopolitan who by carrying the lesson of nature to the
cities would alter the patterns of life they were developing. In short,
Emerson was no Huck Finn turning his back on the facts of modern life
and lighting out for the territory. He was a realist who confronted the
facts of nineteenth-century life but whose vision sprang from the high
expectations of an optimistic Romantic. He was as open to the possibilities of the proper development of the city[17] as he was to the
potentials of machine power and even the factory system.[18] In neither
case, though, would Emerson tolerate the materialism which resulted
in the absurdity of the machine riding humanity, or the city defining
life. Which brings us to a few other pieces in which Emerson celebrates
Man's right relations with nature.

"The Titmouse" (1862), a work of middling length which is composed of conventional iambic tetrameters and utilizes rhymed couplets
throughout, is an easy poem to grasp. In the first stanza the speaker,
revealing his own timidity, immediately expresses the maxim of caution: "You shall not be overbold / When you deal with arctic cold" (*W*,
IX, 233), a lesson which the tiny bird, the titmouse, will belie. In
this first stanza the speaker points up the essential inhospitality of the
"snow-choked wood" through which he is treading and complains of
the numbing effects the "frost-king" is having upon him. The inanimate and deadening quality of the experience is suggested by words
such as "stones" and "marble bones," and the muteness of the opening
stanza is reinforced with effective mortuary language:

> Embalmed by purifying cold;
> The winds shall sing their dead-march old,
> The snow is no ignoble shroud,
> The moon thy mourner, and the cloud.
>
> (*W*, IX, 233)

The silence and heaviness of the scene, however, are happily relieved by the appearance of the bird with its "tiny voice," "Gay and polite." It greets him merrily and expresses a warmth and friendship which are at odds with the speaker's antagonism toward nature. The cheer of the tiny creature is confirmed by the description of its antics; it is "hospitable," courtly, a "feathered lord of land" at "gymnastic play."

Stanza 4 of the narrative begins with the speaker's recounting the lesson he learned from the creature which is a "scrap of valor" that is "Hurling defiance at vast death" (*W*, IX, 234). He recognizes the moral lesson the bird offers and concludes the stanza by observing that in its "titmouse dimension" it offers an admirable model of total communion and harmony with nature. The creature's song, which is translated in stanza 5, is a celebration of a merger with the seemingly inhospitable world.

The last stanza is reflective. The message the speaker carries out of the wood is not merely that spring and renewal are imminent. Rather, like Caesar during the Gallic Wars, he has a "better clew," the "antidote of fear" (*W*, IX, 236). Like the Roman leader, he has come to deserted and forbidding woods, seen the lesson of the bird (which in the first line of stanza 3 is identified as a poet living apart, in the manner of Saadi), and conquered his fear of nature as well as his detachment from it. The bird has taught his lesson well, and our poet has learned it equally well.

Part of the success of "The Titmouse" stems from Emerson's having avoided the sort of gushiness and simplification which so often compromises Romantic nature poetry. Eschewing devices such as the moral tags favored by his contemporaries—for example, the Americans Bryant and Longfellow—Emerson offers a more subtle and integrated message. On the most immediate level, the bird has taught the speaker and the reader a rather obvious, even cliché, lesson. Understood in the broad context of Emerson's Transcendentalism, however, the tiny creature is a paradigm for Man's right relations with the Not Me, precisely the point missed by the Guys of this world, the Bulkeleys and others of

"Hamatreya." The bird is indeed an emblem in homespun whose
meaning is subtly communicated; rather than being boldly and baldly
announced, the poem's meaning flows organically from the narrative
statement.[19]

"Woodnotes" (1840–41) has been judged to be Emerson's "great
comprehensive nature-poem."[20] It is a work of some 460 lines in two
parts and relies almost exclusively on octosyllabic couplets. Perfectly
traditional in its prosody, it is essentially—at least in the form which
Emerson arrived at by the 1876 edition—a celebration of Man's proper
relation to Nature. His affirmations are enhanced by the contrasts
supplied by several passages in which Man's being out of tune with the
cosmos is described. For example, the fifth stanza of "Woodnotes II"
commences with an invitation in the voice of the poet to learn with him
"the fatal song / Which knits the world in music strong." He sustains
the appropriate music metaphor—which he repeatedly sounds when
handling Man's relations with the rest of creation—to the point that
"Nature beats in perfect tune." This is the reality. But at the same time
Man is admonished—"The wood is wiser far than thou" (*W*, IX, 54).
Man, the "poor child! unbound, unrhymed," has somehow in the
evolutionary process been "divorced, deceived and left"; he remains
undernourished, sickly,

> An exile from the wilderness,—
> The hills where health with health agrees,
> And the wise soul expels disease.
> (*W*, IX, 54–55)

In a word—the one Emerson employs in the first line of the sixth
stanza—Man suffers from "bankruptcy" (*W*, IX, 56): moral, spiritual,
emotional, and intellectual. The condition is clearly due to ills such as
the "city's poisoning spleen" which had been cited near the beginning
of stanza 2 of this second section.

But "Woodnotes," both parts, is largely a celebration of Man's right
relation to nature, an exploration of the processes—the surrenders—
necessary for him to establish communion and a description of the
rewards he will enjoy if he does. Slow-paced and, frankly, prolix and
belabored at times, the poem is a Transcendentalist's celebration. Like
the titmouse, the pine tree which serves as the subject of the first line of

"Woodnotes I" and predominates in "Woodnotes II" serves as a unify-
ing symbol and is key in the illumination which takes place. In short,
the lesson offered by the small, commonplace pine—by its very existence and through its hints and bold statements—is crucial to the
enlightenment of the consciousness which engages it.[21] In "Woodnotes" as in other poems the poet is not a shaper of nature but rather a
seer looking into her.[22]

There is no equivocation in Emerson's establishing the poet at home
in the forest. His engagement is simple, physical, and, indeed, Romantic; a "Lover of all things alive," he is a "Wonderer at all he meets, /
Wonderer chiefly at himself" (*W,* IX, 44). At this point the commun-
ing poet is cast in the image of Rousseau's awe-struck child during his
first encounter with the natural world.[23] Section 2 of "Woodnotes I"
further describes the vital connections enjoyed by this "forest seer."
Sensitive to and knowledgeable about virtually all facets of nature, he is
privy to its secrets as well as its revelations, its common and too
frequently overlooked phenomena and occurences. Further, the enchanted, even magical, dimensions of this primal engagement are
suggested. It is, "As if by secret sight he knew / Where, in far fields,
the orchis grew" (*W,* IX, 44).[24] The phallic suggestion implicit in
"orchis" reinforces the vital, vigorous, nonrational dimensions of the
experience. This man is no mere naturalist seeking to classify, no slave
to the Understanding. He is the "pilgrim wise," the "philosopher" (*W,*
IX, 45) who receives the secrets of the partridge, woodcock, thrush,
and hawk—creatures who are only dimly perceived at a distance by
ordinary people.

Prosodically, section 3 of the first part stands unique in the poem.
Setting aside the octosyllabic couplets he relies on for virtually the
entire poem, Emerson moves into chanting pentameters. In tracing the
steps of the forest seer he presents the range and poignancy of his
experience in the direct fashion of the catalogue: the Maine wilderness,
the forest inhabited by the moose, bear, woodpecker, pine. The seer
witnesses the lumberman's felling the noble tree, but unlike the
exploiters of the wood (plunderers such as the rapacious tribe of Aaron
Thousandacres in Cooper's *Chainbearer* and the lumber interests which
laid bare the land Faulkner's Isaac McCaslin had known) Emerson's
"wise man is at home, / His hearth the earth." In nature he is as much
in tune and as reverent as Thoreau, Natty Bumppo, and most of

Romanticism's heroes, especially the Americans. His "clear spirit" is "By God's own light illumined and foreshadowed" (*W*, IX, 46).

Section 4, in which Emerson returns to his ballad measure, climaxes the celebration of Man's harmony in nature. The simple, "musing peasant" who is at the "heart of all the scene" testifies to his utter surrender to the forest and to the spirit which inhabits it. Even in death Mother Nature will embrace, enfold this child as he returns to her arms.

Crucial to the entire poem is the quatrain which introduces "Woodnotes II":

> *As sunbeams stream through liberal space*
> *And nothing jostle or displace,*
> *So waved the pine-tree through my thought*
> *And fanned the dreams it never brought.*
> (*W*, IX, 48; Emerson's italics)

The illumination of the receptive consciousness by this humble and commonplace representative of nature, the pine tree, is strikingly captured by means of the sunbeam reference. The pine beckons and enlightens the man, nourishes and sustains him as the sun's rays warm the world. This earth-rooted creature announces the democracy so central to Emerson's thought: "The rough and bearded forester / Is better than the lord" (*W*, IX, 49). Further, in the evolution of humanity and spirit—creation in general—"The lord is the peasant that was, / The peasant the lord that shall be" (*W*, IX, 49). But vitality, youth, vigor are, at least for the time being, the peasant's. In the second stanza the tree announces the services it offers to him who will exist in harmony with it. More important, of course, is the moral and spiritual sustenance it promises the person who eschews the distorting and corrupting influences of the civilized world which his race has created, and embraces the pristine and virtuous natural world: "Into that forester shall pass . . . power and grace." The Mother will protect the "formidable innocence" of her child (*W*, IX, 50–51).

The ecstasy of the wood-god's song intensifies in the third stanza as it offers the "mystic song / Chanted when the sphere was young." Time and space are suspended as the "paean," the song of thanksgiving, rises, "swells." And we are brought back to the "genesis," "The rushing metamorphosis" when fixed nature dissolves and "Melts things that be to things that seem, / And solid nature to a dream." The "chorus of the ancient Causes" (*W,* IX, 52), however, may not be heard by ordinary mortals whose ears are of stone. Only the pure—the surrendering, transcending seers—may hear it.

The song nears its crescendo as we are invited to compose with the pine a "nobler rhyme." Despite the nationalistic note Emerson injects near the beginning of stanza 4—"Only thy Americans / Can read thy line, can meet thy glance" (*W,* IX, 53)—the condition the pine has celebrated knows no national boundaries.

In stanza 5, after describing in scorning terms the plight, the tragedy of most people, who are out of tune with the cosmos, Emerson chants the virtues and advantages of the person who will fall into harmony with it and "outsee seers, and outwit sages." The external truth is that "A divine improvisation, / From the heart of God proceeds." Forever evolving, the "eternal Pan" reincarnates itself in "new forms" (*W,* IX, 57–58). In describing the Deity in this last and longest stanza of the poem, Emerson reaches for a variety of metaphors: He is the pourer of the precious, nourishing beverage; He is the life-bearing bee, the wide-ranging sheep. Finally, at the end of the pine's increasingly mystical chant, Emerson slips into the abstractions, metaphors, and paradoxes traditional to the explanations of mystics, theologians, and poets:

> ["]Thou metest him by centuries,
> And lo! he passes like the breeze;
> Thou seek'st in globe and galaxy,
> He hides in pure transparency;
> Thou askest in fountains and in fires,
> He is the essence that inquires.
> He is the axis of the star;
> He is the sparkle of the spar;
> He is the heart of every creature;
> He is the meaning of each feature;
> And his mind is the sky.
> Than all it holds more deep, more high."
> (*W,* IX, 59)

The nonrational dimension which Emerson has delved into here is impossible to reduce to rational terms. The Transcendental experience he attempts to verbalize plummets to earth the moment it is penetrated and collapsed to ordinary, comprehensible terms. Riddling is evident from the questions posed throughout the poem.[25] How often does wisdom reside in the poignant and penetrating, if unanswerable, question? How frequently is the wise answer in fact a puzzle? Which brings us to the riddle of "The Sphinx."

Emerson's regard for "The Sphinx" (1841) was probably best expressed by his using it as the lead poem in his first collection. Certainly one of his most enduring poems, and probably one of his greatest, "The Sphinx" should be viewed as an expression of the poet's conception of himself as riddler—a revealer of whatever truth he perceives and reports by means of paradox—and as an exploration of the "disjunction between man and nature."[26]

First published in 1841, the poem is more mystical and baffling than most of Emerson's more difficult verse. The sense of eternity and timelessness which emerges near the end of "Woodnotes II" is apparent from the first stanza of "The Sphinx." From time immemorial, while the ages have "slumbered and slept," the drowsy Sphinx has awaited the seer who will reveal her secret to her. The eternal questions are posed: "'The fate of the man-child, / The meaning of man.'" Man is the culminating and most apparent creature, the fruit or upshot of the "unknown"—the force, spirit, motive—at the center of the cosmos. And the scheme or plan which has produced him is Daedalian, one of cunning artifice. The life cycle is called forth in the second quatrain of the stanza: "Out of sleeping a waking"—nonentity and being are not appropriate substitutes for these metaphors, from the Transcendental point of view—and then back to sleep; death, at least physical death, overtakes life, which is itself another layer of mystery, or "deep," beneath the first (*W,* IX, 20).

Beginning with stanza 3, Emerson rehearses the harmony of creation. The palm, elephant, thrush, waves, breezes, atoms exist in mutual and perfect unity, inspirited by the universal being "By one music enchanted, / One deity stirred." The human dimension emerges in stanza 6. The babe appears; the Rousseauistic child of conventional Romanticism, even of Platonism, is "bathèd in joy" and "Without cloud, in its eyes" (*W,* IX, 21). Naturally, it functions and flourishes on a harmonious, integrated, and nonrational level, basking in an essential and all-too-often ignored sustainer of life itself, such as the sun.

But in the next stanza Man out of tune with the cosmos appears; he "crouches and blushes, / Absconds and conceals"—"An oaf, an accomplice, / He poisons the ground" (*W,* IX, 22). In stanza 8 the sphinx asks who is responsible for Man's fallen state, the "sadness and madness" from which her boy suffers. The analysis—if it might be called such—of the poet commences in stanza 9. First he blames the "Lethe of Nature": While Man's soul might see or sense perfection and long for a harmonious sharing with the universal spirit which inhabits the rest of creation, animate and inanimate, he nevertheless cannot effect his natural desire: "his eyes seek in vain." Perhaps, the poet suggests, the perfection he instinctively seeks is out of reach; life is in fact a series of plateaus, spires, ever-evolving circles, the attainment of one inevitably leading him to desire the next "vision profounder" which once found he will spurn in his desire for "new heavens" (*W,* IX, 23). In his attempt to explain, or at least understand, this poet admits that he himself suffers from the condition and wishes, for example, that his lover were more noble than to settle on him as the object of affection, attraction, aspiration. The flux, the flow, the unceasing evolution of the cosmos are expressed succinctly with "Eterne alternation." The reassurance of Transcendental faith, however, is offered: "Love works at the centre, / Heart-heaving alway" (*W,* IX, 23–24).

The ultimate meaning of the poem does not lie in the all-too-facile explanations of this poet. Rather, it resides in the concluding four stanzas in which the poet—who is not to be identified with Emerson—concludes his answer to the sphinx; she in turn responds; and the narrator-poet—who is close to Emerson if not him—forms what conclusion he can from what he reports as having transpired.

There is clearly an underlying superciliousness and an almost comic self-confidence in the reductive simplicity in the answer of the poet—who is not to be confused with the narrator-poet.[27] It is captured tersely in his conclusion, where he addresses her as "Dull Sphinx" and observes that her "sight is growing blear" (*W,* IX, 24)—recall the babe's clarity of vision, noted above. He even presumes to prescribe the remedy "Her muddy eyes to clear!" The sphinx, the eternal symbol of silent wisdom, rebukes the insolent, even arrogant fellow who would reduce mystery to logical explanation. The point is that what she reveals is not at all clear. Her statement does not unequivocally answer or attempt to correct the poet's explanation. What insight revealed by Reason can ever be so expressed? Rather the sphinx turns the question on him: You yourself, poet, are the "unanswered question" and if you are capable of seeing that, keep asking it, even though you will know beforehand that each successive answer will in fact be a lie. The signs of wisdom are awe in the face of the mystery, appropriate humility and respect.

If the merry poet is not capable of recognizing the justice of the sphinx's good-humored assault on his explanation, the narrator—presumably Emerson—is more than able. For him the sphinx soars into symbol; she and her message inspirit, illuminate, and in fact merge with the representatives of physical actuality—some startling, some commonplace, but all finally wondrous by virtue of her: stone, cloud, moon, flame, blossom, wave, and mountain. She herself becomes the poet and offers hope to Mankind: " 'Who telleth one of my meanings / Is master of all I am' " (W, IX, 25)—and the telling simply cannot be on the common-sense level of the Understanding. Rationalism, the curse of modern Man, is the cause of his being out of harmony with the cosmos. Reason, the nonrational, is the way to wisdom. This is the secret shared by the sphinx and the genuine poet—the poet as distinct from the verse-maker. As *Dichter, vates,* the inspired and wise speaker of riddles, the poet offers truth—reality—and also secures to the degree possible a right relation to the baffling mysteries of the universe and existence.[28]

The variety of Emerson's response to the natural world would not be appreciated were the reader to ignore the joyful lightness of the colloquial, homespun narrative of "The Adirondacs" (1867), a work which reflects his later mellowness and stands in contrast to his Transcendental madness. On its most elementary level the poem records the pleasure experienced by Emerson and his fellows in the Adirondack Club during the 1850s. In recounting the holiday of 1858, he celebrates in a fashion almost cliché the beauty and serenity of the wilderness and the group's shared sense of relief from everyday, insubstantial cares. This is the voice of homespun, laced with a keen sense of the comic:

> Hard fare, hard bed and comic misery,—
> The midge, the blue-fly and the mosquito
> Painted our necks, hands, ankles, with red bands.
> (W, IX, 188)

Reading even on this level, however, one has to wince at the incongruity, even fatuousness of the joy with which the Transcendentalist reports the vacationers' response to the news that the transatlantic cable has finally been laid. The importance of whether the Princess Adelaide has the whooping cough, the poignant and pointed question raised by Thoreau earlier in the decade,[29] seems of no concern to our speaker in stanzas 17 and 18. Rather, there is a certain resignation—one has to strain too hard to capture an ironic tone—as he accepts his own and his fellows' limited horizons, their apparent inability or lack of desire to engage nature with other than the Understanding. The crowd included the naturalist Louis Agassiz and the comparative anatomist Jeffries Wyman.[30] Stanza 19 commences:

> We flee away from cities, but we bring
> The best of cities with us, these learned classifiers,
> Men knowing what they seek, armed eyes of experts.
> (*W,* IX, 193)

The holidays end and civilization intrudes as it simply could not upon the genuine Transcendental experiences he had recorded a decade or two earlier:

> And Nature, the inscrutable and mute,
> Permitted on her infinite repose
> Almost a smile to steal to cheer her sons,
> As if one riddle of the Sphinx were guessed.
> (*W,* IX, 194)

It is not unfair to suggest that the sense of mystery held forth by the Sphinx of the earlier poem is at best tolerantly alluded to here; it seems no longer to be really desired. As in poems such as "Monadnoc" (1847), "Musketaquid" (1847), "Waldeinsamkeit" (1858), and "May-Day" (1867), the sense of mystery and awe is absent, the bardic chants have been abandoned. In this poem a mellower, warmer Emerson, now fifty-five, offers us a Romantic tenderfoot's sensual experience; absent is the burning need for Reason to command and transcendence to occur. The lesson of the guides, the wilderness men of stanzas 7 and 8, is less a model of engagement with nature and of pristine virtue than a home-spun alternative to the perfectly acceptable ways of life of the "polished gentlemen," the "Ten scholars" (W, IX, 184–85) in whose company Emerson enjoys his recreation. In short, the civilized and the wilderness seem to have been reconciled in the glow of late middle age.

Not all of Emerson's poetry concerns Man's relations with nature or the art of the poet. Among what promise to be the more enduring works, there are several which contemplate and speak to the issues which gave rise to the Civil War, and several others which articulate deeply felt personal experiences, notably the death of his son Waldo. In addition there is a small gathering of poems for public occasions, the best of which is the "Concord Hymn."

The work Emerson placed last in his first collection, "Concord Hymn" was first sung at the celebration marking the completion of the Revolutionary War battle monument on which it is carved. A public, patriotic utterance, first delivered on July 4, 1837, the poem stands— and rightly so—as one of the most memorable of its genre. Composed of four quatrains in octosyllabics, it begins with an inspiring tribute to the "embattled farmers" who "fired the shot heard round the world"—one of Emerson's better remembered lines. The second stanza notes the passage of time and the attending change which has been wrought; the third focuses on the events of the commemoration; and the final quatrain sings the message which is the principal purpose of the poem: "Bid Time and Nature gently spare / The shaft we raise" (W, IX, 158–59). The most remarkable quality of this dignified public poem is its restraint, its controlled emotion and skillful avoidance of mawkish patriotism.

Slavery is one of the thematic groupings in which we find some excellent poems as well as some of moderate success. The "Ode: Inscribed to W. H. Channing" (1847) has as its primary concern the materialism which informed the political arena inhabited by Daniel Webster. The poem employs tight, emotionally charged dimeters and trimeters and what is best described as erratic rhyming, both of which communicate the intensity of Emerson's feelings on the subject. The first two stanzas in effect apologize for or justify the distance Emerson chose to keep from the political fray. Neither the "priest's cant" nor the "statesman's rant" will force him to abandon his "honied thought." Indeed, if he leaves his study "The angry Muse / Puts confusion in [his] brain." Emerson will simply not raise the specter of compromise, which would open the possibility of his wavering from a position of principle.

Following this self-justification, the voice launches into an angry, actually sneering, attack on Webster. It commences with a rhetorical question regarding the master politician's empty and foolish lip service to "the culture of mankind, / Of better arts and life?" This is unconscionable prating at a time the expansionist government in its hunger for territory is "Harrying Mexico" (*W*, IX, 76). More malign than the shortsighted and foolish men of "Guy" and "Hamatreya," these materialists are cut from the same cloth as the "jackals" who hold slaves, "little men" before whom "Virtue palters; Right is hence; / Freedom praised, but hid" (*W*, IX, 77). Reptilian imagery, carrying reference to the betrayal in the Eden myth, winds throughout the poem: "blindworm," "snake," even "stolen fruit." But the climax of Emerson's moral censure and contempt comes in stanzas 6 and 7,[31] which conclude with two of his most memorable lines: "Things are in the saddle, / And ride mankind." The upshot of this gross and callous materialism is that man is unkinged, the "law for thing[s] . . . runs wild" (*W*, IX, 78). Expansion, commerce, development, and exploitation have become ends in and of themselves. The tone of the last two stanzas is more restrained, prophetic. Emerson is not calling upon the "wrinkled shopman" to commune with nature, nor is he asking the powerful senator to "Ask votes of thrushes in the solitudes" (*W*, IX, 79). Rather, with the calm assurance of the reflecting and principled Transcendentalist, he is predicting that Freedom will carry the war if not the battle. Flux, change, balance, compensation will right the wrongs. Ultimately, the affairs of the nation will be in the hands of leaders and followers who will be better than the "little men" with whom "The God who made New Hampshire [has] / Taunted the lofty land" (*W*, IX, 77).

The depth of Emerson's feelings on these matters might be measured by considering "Webster" (1884), part of the Phi Beta Kappa poem he had delivered at Harvard in 1834; it is interesting and valuable principally as an expression of the poet's earlier admiration of the dominating public figure who is "cast in the heroic mould / Of them who rescued liberty of old." A spokesman for "the conscience of the country" (*W*, IX, 398), he is a model of common sense and public virtue—a statesman rather than a mere politician. But seventeen years later, in May 1851, as Emerson's distress over the debate surrounding the "peculiar institution" intensified, he denounced the Fugitive Slave Law as well as Webster and the other political compromisers who had supported its passage. Labeling the act "filthy," he vowed, "I will not obey it, by God!" (*JMN*, XI, 412).

The "Boston Hymn," which Emerson read in Boston's Music Hall on New Year's Day 1863, in the aftermath of the Emancipation Proclamation, marks the intensity of his response during the War. Simple and clear in its language and statement, aimed at a wide audience similar to those he tried to touch with his lectures, it is patriotic and emotional, altogether a public utterance. Appropriately enough for the time and place, he begins by recalling the divine imperative which had been carried out nearly two and a half centuries earlier by the Pilgrims. Then, for the remainder of the poem he reports in the hymn's Common Meter on the assertions or directives of the Deity who will no longer suffer kings and tyrants who "Might harry the weak and poor" (*W*, IX, 201). Freedom is His angel; and Freedom has informed what progress and achievement there have been. There is a toughness, an uncompromising bitterness here which was virtually unheard in the Emerson of the 1850s. In the most moving sections of the poem, stanzas 10 through 16, he chants his democratic faith and raises images of a rough-hewn brotherhood working together in mutual respect and harmony. Stanzas 17 through 21 focus on the violation of the ideal he has envisioned by the slavocracy which was collapsing, and the last stanza offers an image of an angry God who warns that His "will fulfilled shall be" and that His "thunderbolt has eyes to see / His way home to the mark" (*W*, IX, 204). What this seemingly occasional poem said to its period audience is perhaps less important than what it reveals of Emerson's development by the early 1860s. Absent from the platform is the man who some twenty years earlier announced that "evil is merely privative." Evil is indeed very real and shall be avenged, not by a beneficent and loving God, but by an angry Deity. Given its purpose and occasion, the "Boston Hymn" should endure as well as any similar pieces by his contemporaries, including Whittier.

A few poems which should continue to stand the test of time are autobiographical and reveal the deep stress to which Emerson was subjected during his great creative period in the 1830s and 1840s.

"Threnody" (1847), one of his most personal utterances, is an elegy which bares the emotional pain he suffered when his five-year-old son, Waldo, died early in 1842; it is also a remarkable illustration of the fervor and depth of the poet's Transcendentalism. A fine example of the binary form he favored, the first part sounds the poet's lament and the second expresses what reconciliation, if not consolation, the "deep Heart" offers to assuage the singer's wound. Neither the poem nor the philosophical acceptance of the child's death which it chants was hastily or easily won, as is evident from the slow and difficult development of its sentiments in the journals and letters of the period.

The poem, which is for the most part composed in Emerson's favorite octosyllabic couplets, begins by announcing without irony that, in effect, April is indeed the cruellest month. There is literally no distinction between Emerson and a persona as he reports that the South-wind cannot alter the passing of Waldo, "The darling who shall not return" (*W*, IX, 148). The poet's anguish is expressed in the commonplace realities—the "empty house"—and vital recollections—Waldo's "silver warble wild"—with which he is left. Most effective in the second stage, and pertinent to the entire poem, is the language of the pulsing, dazzling life which he uses to describe the "wondrous child," the "hyacinthine boy" (*W*, IX, 148). Stanza 3 asks, among other questions, where the boy is and recalls the enchanting effect he had on the lives he touched, and the next two stanzas are even more specific as Emerson recollects the lad's activities and confronts the emblems of him which remain: the "painted sled," "gathered sticks," "The ominous hole he dug in the sand" (*W*, IX, 151). And then he offers what becomes an intense and bewildered account of the uninterrupted natural process, which leads him into the transitional passage in which he questions whether there might have been a "watcher," an "angel," in the universe which "Could stoop to heal that only child, / Nature's sweet marvel undefiled" (*W*, IX, 152). There follows a long section of introspection and a search for philosophical and psychological distinction in which the mourner wonders if, indeed, "Perchance not he but Nature ailed, / The world and not the infant failed." Perhaps the world "was not ripe yet to sustain / A genius of so fine a strain." The eighth stanza, which concludes the first part of the poem, reveals a despairing, confused, and bitter speaker, a man "too much bereft" who can only chant:

> O truth's and nature's costly lie!
> O trusted broken prophecy!
> O richest fortune sourly crossed!
> (*W*, IX, 154)

The next two stanzas present the answer of the "deep Heart" which begins with a stern though not scolding response to the anguish of the grieving parent. There is no reason to question Emerson's sincerity in describing the wisdom which sustains him during this period of terrible loss, although readers who seem more emotional than philosophical might wonder at the toughness of the reconciliation. It was a reconciliation, however, won after great difficulty and should even be viewed as an ultimate test of the bereaved father's Transcendental faith. (He addressed the problem in the essay "Experience" [see pp. 58–60, above], which explains some of the thinking necessary to understand the poem.) Beneath his stoicism lies the foundation of compensation and the many other supports of the philosophical system—if it may be labeled such—Emerson had constructed. The wisdom born of speculation and experience was not only hard won but genuine. In a moment of severest test, the death of a loved one—one of the several losses he had endured—the underpinnings he had placed served him well. He did not collapse.

The statement of the "Heart" in "Threnody" is conventionally Emersonian. It asks, "But thou, my votary, weepest thou? / I gave thee sight—where is it now?" (*W*, IX, 155). There is a reason, although it is beyond Man's ability to grasp it. The tone of the Heart softens, however, in the final stanza as it calls the mourner's attention to the larger process, the inevitable flux, of nature and then asks two poignant, rhetorical questions, positive answers to which would be absurd:

> Wilt thou freeze love's tidal flow,
> Whose streams through Nature circling go?
> Nail the wild star to its track
> On the half-climbed zodiac?
> (*W*, IX, 156)

Change is at the center of the evolving universe, change from which nothing can escape. Emerson relies on a group of organic metaphors to define this evolution born of flux: "bending reeds, / Flowering grass and scented weeds" (*W*, IX, 157). If this cannot be reduced to rational terms, to the context of Understanding, so much the better. It is in fact a matter of Reason, of faith; the poet is admonished to "Revere the Maker," who rushes silently "Through ruined systems still restored."

Appropriately enough, the paradox of the last line—"Lost in God, in Godhead found"—is introduced by the images of death and larger vision which are joined in the two preceding lines of the poem: "Apples of Eden ripe to-morrow. / House and tenant go to ground" (*W,* IX, 157–58).

The stoicism and organicism of "Threnody" offer one avenue to the appreciation of "Give All to Love" (1847). One senses the same depth of feeling here as in the lament for the dead Waldo. After describing in rather abstract terms the intensity of the emotion and the rightness of surrender, Emerson cautions, "Yet, hear me, yet" (*W,* IX, 91). Anticipate, prepare for her fleeing by accepting it and recognizing that despite the immediate and apparent pain which the beloved's departure causes, her leaving is natural, even inevitable. Rightly understood, it is even an occasion for rejoicing for new insight: "When half-gods go"— that is, earthly love departs—"The gods arrive" (*W,* IX, 92) with their wisdom born of Reason. Stoic perhaps even to the point of coldness, the sentiment is from the same Transcendental fabric as that of "Threnody."

There is no more fitting work than "Terminus" with which to end this discussion of Emerson's poetry. Although it was collected in *May-Day and Other Pieces* in 1867, it probably was composed in the 1850s, shortly after the burst of poetic activity which preceded the publication of the first collection of poems. "Terminus" is a weary and gentle poem,[32] movingly honest and, it seems, overly modest in its assessment of Emerson's own gifts and accomplishments.[33] The fires which had ignited his imagination are at least banked. The poem commences with a lamentation that "It is time to be old, / To take in sail," and he announces that what power has inspired him, "The god of bounds," has ordered him

> "No more!
> No farther shoot
> Thy broad ambitious branches, and thy root[."]
> (*W,* IX, 251)

The organic metaphor is appropriate; the sense of limit and failing potential is scarcely redeemed by the suggestion that the poet will "Mature the unfallen fruit," perhaps such poems as "The Adirondacs" and "The Titmouse." More touching and disturbing is the sense of failure which concludes the first stanza. Of course, Emerson is referring to his lineage here, but more important he is describing his own ambivalence, his suspension, which caused his lack of success "Amid the gladiators" of the world of action as well as "Amid the Muses" who left him "deaf and dumb" (*W,* IX, 252). This is not merely false modesty, a clever if transparent bid for contradiction by the reader, but it might betray a disturbing lack of comprehension of his achievement, or it might even suggest that the piece was composed during a period of deep depression. The bleakness of the poem is scarcely redeemed by the resignation one hears in the last stanza—"I trim myself to the storm of time"—or by the stoic fortitude recommended by the words of the god which conclude the poem:

> "Lowly faithful, banish fear,
> Right onward drive unharmed;
> The port, well worth the cruise, is near,
> And every wave is charmed."
> (*W,* IX, 252)

The number of Emerson's poems which have endured, and those which might continue to, may be modest. But then, aside from the giants of English poetry who reign as strongly today as they have in the past centuries—Chaucer, Shakespeare, Milton certainly—is Emerson's achievement significantly less than that of others in the second and third tiers of the English poetic tradition? Probably not. Although one early critic undoubtedly overstated the case when he suggested that Emerson's poetry would probably outlast his prose,[34] among American poets Emerson does deserve, by virtue of those remarkably intense and technically accomplished works discussed in this chapter, to hold a place equal to that of our dozen most important poets. At least, to cite a cliché among students of American Romanticism, if Emerson is "not our greatest writer," he is "our only inescapable one . . . . Denied or scorned, he turns up again in every opponent, however orthodox, classical, conservative or even just Southern."[35] True as this less than faint praise may be—and it is perhaps a strategy of defense which the reader should hear with irony—the fact remains that Emerson at his best gave us some of our finest poems.

Chapter Five

Sky of Law, Pismire of Performance

The decade framed by the publication of *Representative Men* (1850) and *The Conduct of Life* (1860) might be described as having wrought significant changes in certain aspects of Emerson's thinking; however, it seems more accurate to understand this period as bringing forth new balances and fresh emphases in his thought. Some critics have generalized about his newly emerged perspectives by using labels such as skepticism, fatalism, and acquiescence. But such terms should not suggest that during this later middle period there were wholesale departures from his earlier Transcendental assertions, or even repudiations of them. Whicher's response, for instance, to the development of Emerson's views is at once sympathetic and harsh. Describing the dissolving of Emerson's initial "Saturnalia of faith" as "a defeat that laid a shadow of promise unfulfilled across his later serenity," Whicher, who was writing in the early 1950s, found what he characterizes as Emerson's "comprehensive acceptance . . . [to be] more irritating than helpful in our disastrous times." Yet it is hard to understand how any intelligent and rational human being, even one of Emerson's "millennial expectations," could hope to sustain in maturity his "dreams of a Messianic greatness."[1] Rather it appears that the seeds of his skepticism and acquiescence, to use Whicher's language, were there from early in the career. In the middle period, from the early 1840s to about 1860, they were more center-stage in the drama of his intellectual life, but not entirely because of his disenchantment with his visions of Man's potential. Philosophical skepticism and a sense of Fate—even in the early, visionary period—were as much in his thought, although he emphasized his belief in the possibilities of the individual. Perhaps they are best explained as being reflective of his seemingly innate hospitality to opposites, his naturally dialectical intellectual style. Then again, one might say that as he matured, as he stepped away from the early and necessary confrontations with establishments such as the Harvard Divinity School, his more temperate and less passionate self began to emerge, its dictates becoming stronger as the 1840s and 1850s unfolded. For whatever combination of reasons, there were new emphases in this middle period. They might even be viewed as logical extensions of avenues he had been exploring almost from the beginning.

Celebration of the individual's potential and his moral authority was, of course, central to Emerson's early vision and is perhaps one of the most captivating aspects of his thought. As we have seen, however, the equally important and related ideas of development and growth—process, in a word—lie at the heart of *Essays: First Series* and were further emphasized in *Essays: Second Series*. As personal difficulties and the more public problems of the young Republic loomed larger and more pressing for him, Emerson sustained his optimism by adopting a broader view which diminished the importance of the dark present he lived in and emphasized hope for the future. Such is the strategy of "Politics" in *Essays: Second Series*. If in the early 1840s he had little faith in the bellowings of the politicos and the judgments of the masses, he was nevertheless convinced that "beneficent necessity" (*W*, III, 212) would continue to float the not altogether efficient raft of state. And in the 1850s, when the political, economic, and social picture darkened as Americans scrambled for power, position, and authority, and Emerson became even more discouraged about the dismal times, he came to emphasize the themes of melioration and the better future. After all, the visionary, assertive prophet of self-reliance had recognized in the early period that the incursions of Reason into the individual soul were rare and holy events. As the antebellum decade unfolded, his description of these moments of individual transcendence and, it seems, his concern with them, became even rarer.

As his earlier focus shifted, new emphases on determinism, relativism, and process emerged. His new insistencies undoubtedly sprang from personal psychological factors—an increasing sense that his powers were declining[2]—but they were also brought on by the bleakness he observed in modern life, particularly in America. He had always confronted and derided his contemporaries' materialism and baseness of means and ends, what he judged to be the young nation's failure of vision. But in the 1850s he sensed that these misdirections were capturing the culture with a vengeance. An abiding belief in process, melioration, and hope for the future were the best means available to the middle-age Transcendentalist to comprehend the mad scramble put in motion by fluid and volatile politics; industrial, economic, and geographical expansion; and rapidly changing social, moral, and ethical values. These prewar years were terribly difficult for Emerson, but rather than seeing them as signaling the collapse of American culture and the dream it was purportedly to realize, he viewed the period as a necessary step in the evolutionary process. For the time being, he and his culture must contend with life-denying, ugly forces such as those which would extend slavery to the frontier territories and those which would manipulate economic markets and political processes in high-stakes, open-ended free-for-alls. Emerson understood as well as anyone in public life that the ordered, relatively simple, and predictable world of the early century was gone, replaced by the raucous, rough-and-tumble arenas of commerce, law, and politics, for example, in which new ethics, even new moralities, were being forged. There was little if any time to describe much less seek the Transcendental seer, to propose models of conduct to a tough, pragmatic society on the move. Heroes were marked by blemishes, which were better analyzed and understood than ignored or cosmetized.

In the writings of the 1850s there are no ideal, self-reliant heroes, transcending seers of the sort he had described early in the 1840s. Probably because of the observations he had made and the experience he had gained—for example, in the political arena—during the fluid and volatile antebellum decade and earlier, he attempts to record, comprehend, and perhaps even shape to better advantage the times' realities. He is less—if at all—concerned with offering visions. *Representative Men* is a case in point. In being representative these figures are symbolic, not models of conduct which he is holding up for emulation, much less worship. Nor is he offering jeremiads. The subjects of his penetrating analyses are men who stand for certain universal values or ideas that their own times and cultures dictated. Equally important, they were flawed in that they were incomplete, possessed critical limitations, and suffered failures of behavior and vision.

By the time he published *Representative Men* in 1850, Emerson had been lecturing for years on the subject. The overview chapter, "Uses of Great Men," which opens the volume, sets forth the principal advantages and potential liabilities which in his judgment should guide any reader in the study of the lives of the great—the heroes in myth and legend, the gods of fable. One senses an implicit pragmatism in the very suggestion that we "use" great men. These giants are "lenses through which we read our own minds," seers who dwell on "a higher sphere of thought" (*W*, IV, 5–6). In short, they command attention because they are representative or symbolic of things or ideas. However, the power they "communicate is not theirs" but belongs, for example, to the idea which they embody; even Plato is a "debtor" (*W*, IV, 19) in the sense that any "man is a centre for nature, running out threads of relation through every thing" (*W*, IV, 9).

Emerson warns that the student, like the American scholar of the late 1830s, must not be overwhelmed, eclipsed: "True genius will not impoverish, but will liberate, and add new senses" (*W*, IV, 18). The individual and his present are ever at the center. Great men "clear our eyes from egotism and enable us to see other people and their works" (*W*, IV, 25); not only do these historical personages protect us from the excessive influence of our contemporaries, but encourage our precious self-reliance if they are viewed in proper perspective.

For the reality is that "Every hero becomes a bore at last" (*W*, IV, 27) and, further, in the scheme of things even the great person will be balanced by his opposite. So as each person naturally seeks to preserve and protect his individuality, he will benefit from the "power of the greatest men" as "their spirit diffuses itself. . . . in concentric circles" (*W*, IV, 33). The great person serves a purpose in the ascent of existence and in the end "he appears as an exponent of a vaster mind and will." A sort of medium, he encourages the "opaque self" of the one who studies him to become "transparent with the light of the First Cause" (*W*, IV, 34–35).

It is clear that this was one of the principal benefits Emerson derived from his long study of "Plato; or, the Philosopher," the first subject of the six chronologically arranged biographies in the volume. Disposing in one paragraph of the "external biography" (*W*, IV, 43), Emerson concentrates—as he would for each of his subjects—on the substance and significance of the interior life of this fountainhead of European thought. Having "absorbed the learning of his times" (*W*, IV, 42), Plato is remarkable in having synthesized and enhanced both East and West, wedded "The unity of Asia and the detail of Europe; the infinitude of the Asiatic soul and the defining, result-loving, machine-making, surface-seeking, opera-going Europe" (*W*, IV, 53–54). Capturing the excellence of both, he brought forth the "balanced soul" (*W*, IV, 54) and transferred nature's synthesis to Man's consciousness. Plato's was the "arrival of accuracy and intelligence" (*W*, IV, 47). His was the ability, in a word, to "define"; he left "with Asia the vast and superlative" (*W*, IV, 47), the religious tendency toward Unity in contrast to the Western intellectual penchant toward diversity. Despite his defects of expressing himself in a literary way and lacking a system, Plato possessed an enormous "common-sense" (*W*, IV, 61) and taught humanity that "[']things are knowable!'" (*W*, IV, 62). Though this philosopher "never writes in ecstasy, or catches us up in poetic raptures" (*W*, IV, 61), he saw that "[']All things are symbolical; and what we call results are beginnings'" (*W*, IV, 68). In other words, he understood the mounting ascension—the melioration—of things. Flux, relativity, Emerson assures us again, are inevitable since no one ever has or ever will have "the smallest success in explaining existence. The perfect enigma [always] remains" (*W*, IV, 78).

And so with the other subjects discussed in the volume. Of the caste of men "divine" who give us a glimpse of "the secrets and structure of nature by some higher method than by experience" (*W*, IV, 95), Swedenborg is one who had "*ecstasy* or absence,—a getting out of their bodies to think" and achieved "beatitude" (*W*, IV, 97) by passing "the bounds of space and time . . . into the dim spirit-realm" (*W*, IV, 101). He is among humanity's lawgivers by virtue of his "moral insight" (*W*, IV, 124), but his perception was "narrowed and defeated" (*W*, IV, 120), his genius "wasted. . . . by attaching [itself] to the Christian symbol, instead of to the moral sentiment" (*W*, IV, 135); and so he became a passionless classifier. Although he was blessed with the gift of mystical insight, Swedenborg was thwarted by the strictures of inherited, prescribed forms and did not achieve the freedom, the self-reliance, which is imperative for genuine insight.

In a similar fashion, Shakespeare, however successful he was, shared "the halfness and imperfection of humanity" (*W*, IV, 216), and so we still seek the "poet-priest . . . who shall see, speak, and act, with equal inspiration" (*W*, IV, 219) and celebrate the universe and life. Like Plato, and for that matter virtually any great person, including the moderns, Napoleon and Goethe, Shakespeare's "Genius" was "forced onward by the ideas and necessities of his contemporaries" (*W*, IV, 189–90). Napoleon, the "incarnate Democrat" (*W*, IV, 224), the bane of conservative establishments, is another "[']creature of circumstances'" (*W*, IV, 232), born because the times required him. No ordinary representative of this "active, brave" (*W*, IV, 224), upwardly mobile middle class, he was a practical workman who added "insight and generalization" (*W*, IV, 229) to his gifts. Yet however appropriate this "thoroughly modern" man may be for the rapidly changing nineteenth century (Emerson notes his own country's penchant for embracing and emulating Bonapartes), he was "no hero, in the high sense" (*W*, IV, 225), and his "experiment" was doomed to inevitable failure because his aim was merely "sensual and selfish" (*W*, IV, 258). Despite his intellectual prowess, his ability to work his arithmetic in order to shape events, he was as incapable of integrating life as his near contemporary, Goethe, "the philosopher of this multiplicity" which marks the modern age. Able to pierce the nineteenth century's "rolling miscellany of facts and sciences" (*W*, IV, 271), Goethe, like Napoleon, "set the axe at the root of the tree of cant and seeming" (*W*, IV, 289). As an artist, however, he failed because he was "fragmentary; a writer of occasional poems and of an encyclopaedia of sentences" (*W*, IV, 287).

"Montaigne; or, the Skeptic" signals the direction and style of Emerson's most important thought during the decade. Skepticism was one of the major avenues he followed. He begins the essay by observing and challenging the tendency people have to view life and the universe through the particular lens to which they are predisposed. Generally, there are "The abstractionist and the materialist" (*W*, IV, 154), for example, the poets and philosophers, on the one hand, and the practical "men of toil and trade and luxury" (*W*, IV, 151), on the other. In its arrogance each group rejects the version of reality proposed and, admittedly, insisted upon by the other.

The skeptic occupies the "middle ground between these two" extremists; like any of his breed, as understood in classic and modern philosophy, the skeptic, standing suspended, denies certitude. "He finds both [abstractionists and materialists] wrong by being in extremes. He labors to plant his feet, to be the beam of the balance. . . . He sees the one-sidedness of these men of the street. . . . he stands for the intellectual faculties, a cool head and whatever serves to keep it cool. . . . You that will have all solid, and a world of pig-lead, deceive yourselves grossly" (*W,* IV, 155). In its essentials, this posture is no different from Emerson's reluctance from the very beginning of his career to accept one orthodoxy or another. Viewed positively, it is the same openness and flexibility which lay behind his earlier challenges to institutions—the academic and Divinity School establishments, conventional historiography, even reform movements, for instance—and his insistence on flux, relativism, and melioration in earlier writings: essays such as "History," "Self-Reliance," "The Over-Soul," "Circles," "Intellect," "Experience," "Politics," and "Nominalist and Realist" as well as poems such as "The Sphinx" and "Threnody." This philosophical skepticism is at the heart of his hospitality to diversity and change and is also the source of the most important of his mature thought in the 1850s. The skeptic sees plainly enough to admit that he cannot see. Refusing to pretend that he possesses "powers" and "assurances" which he does not have, and "weary" of "dogmatizers" as well as their opponents, the "hacks of routine, who deny the dogmas," the skeptic neither affirms nor denies but, acknowledging that "There is much to say on all sides," listens (*W,* IV, 156–57). In brief, the skeptic's "right ground" is "not at all of unbelief; not at all of universal denying, nor of universal doubting,—doubting even that he doubts; least of all of scoffing and profligate jeering at all that is stable and good" (*W,* IV, 159). Emerson's skeptic is no Pyrrho and neither is his position to be confused with that of the cynic or the nihilist. Rather, "He is the considerer, the prudent, taking in sail, counting stock, husbanding his means, believing that . . . we cannot give ourselves too many advantages in this unequal conflict, with powers so vast and unweariable ranged on one side, and this little conceited vulnerable popinjay that a man is, bobbing up and down into every danger, on the other" (*W,* IV, 159–60). The self-reliant person confronting the purveyors of absolutes has receded; even the poet, that arch-individualist, that ultimate seer, seems to have dissolved as Emerson wraps himself in a mantle of skepticism; replacing him in the drama of ideas we have the more cautious, questioning, prudent scholar—in a phrase the doubting intellectual.

Emerson moves on to insist that "The philosophy we want is one of fluxions and mobility." Steering a course between the "stark and stiff" and the "thin and aerial," he wants "some coat woven of elastic steel. . . . a ship in these billows we inhabit," rather than "An angular, dogmatic house [which] would be rent to chips and splinters in this storm of many elements" (*W,* IV, 160). To adapt in the face of inevitable challenge is more intelligent than to insist on the absolute validity of one or another version of reality as so many are capable of doing, even to the point of self-destruction.

Recognizing that acceptance or rejection of the skeptic's posture is often a matter of constitution, even of "temperament" (*W,* IV, 181), he suggests that everyone passes through a period of skepticism at some point in life. In a very personal passage, in which the "we" is editorial rather than generic, he admits that "We are natural believers. Truth, or the connection between cause and effect, alone interests us. . . . Seen or unseen, we believe the tie exists. Talent makes counterfeit ties; genius finds the real ones" (*W,* IV, 170). The simple fact, however, is that truth is hard won, if ever grasped. Or as Melville in the same year, 1850, was to say in his review of "Hawthorne and His Mosses": "Innate Depravity and Original Sin, from whose visitations, in some shape or other, no deeply thinking mind is always and wholly free. For, in certain moods, no man can weigh this world, without throwing in something, somehow like Original Sin, to strike the uneven balance."[3] Melville's clever rhetorical strategy may be more forceful, but Emerson is making the same point about skepticism. The "student," performing his necessary function as skeptic, interrogates society's adored customs. The very act of interrogation is "an inevitable stage in the growth of every superior mind, and is the evidence of its perception of the flowing power which remains itself in all changes." This "superior mind," this "skeptic," is necessarily a "bad citizen" by virtue of his refusal to endorse either party, the conservative or democratic. "The dull pray; the geniuses are light mockers" (*W,* IV, 172, 174). There is the possibility that a person might indeed see, but in "Montaigne" Emerson displays a greater reluctance to promise the event than he had in the earlier writings, in passages such as the transparent eye-ball section in *Nature* or in "Self-Reliance." Insight, transcendence, had never been easy; "Reason, the prized reality, the Law, is apprehended, now and then, for a serene and profound moment amidst the hubbub of cares and works which have no direct bearing on it;—is then lost for months or years, and again found for an interval, to be lost again. . . . So vast is the disproportion between the sky of law and the pismire of performance under it, that whether he is a man of worth or a sot is not so great a matter as we say" (*W,* IV, 178–79). The language is strong and down to earth, but there is a weariness and resignation here which even when it appeared in the earlier work was almost always offset by bold announcements, courageous assertions, visions. The essay on Montaigne, though, does conclude with hopefulness, a promise of ultimate melioration. Man must generalize, see beyond that "march of civilization [which] is a train of felonies." Nevertheless, "the world-spirit is a good swimmer, and storms and waves cannot drown him. . . . Through the years and the centuries, through evil agents, through toys and atoms, a great and beneficent tendency irresistibly streams." But if one detects resignation here, there is also a certain confidence that there is "the permanent in the mutable and fleeting." Clinging to his "reverence," Man will "learn that he is here, not to work but to be worked upon; and that, though abyss open under abyss, and opinion displace opinion, all are at last contained in the Eternal Cause:—'If my bark sink, 't is to another sea'" (*W,* IV, 185–86). The former assertiveness, however, has been tempered. There is a pervading sense of powers and forces which Man is not likely to overcome. In brief, there is at the end of the essay a sense of Fate, an aspect of experience he had raised just a few pages earlier: "The word Fate, or Destiny, expresses the sense of mankind, in all ages, that the laws of the world do not always befriend, but often hurt and crush us" (*W,* IV, 177).

Emerson froze in print his most mature thought on the subject ten years later in "Fate," the lead piece in *The Conduct of Life,* but he was lecturing on the subject as early as 1851. The essay offers a concise, frank, and eloquent discussion of a problem which Emerson, like any "deeply thinking mind," in Melville's phrase, had pondered from the time he had become intellectually conscious. The question was particularly bothersome to this man whose time, circumstances, and even temperament had led him to assert the final freedom and authority of the individual with perhaps more vigor, certainty, and conviction than any of his contemporaries—even his fellow Transcendentalists—during the five years following the publication of his first book, *Nature,* almost a quarter-century earlier.

From the first several paragraphs of "Fate" Emerson insists on our necessary obedience to these powers and on our limitations. No longer is he emphasizing and celebrating the self-reliant individual, the Man Thinking, who might mold his own destiny. For example, if we desire to reform men, we must finally recognize that "We must begin . . . at generation: that is to say, there is Fate, or laws of the world" (*W,* VI, 4). This is quite different from his earlier insistence—in "New England Reformers," for example—that were the individual regenerated, there would be no need for institutional reform. The old faith and the abiding optimism nevertheless remain: "If we must accept Fate, we are not less compelled to affirm liberty, the significance of the individual, the grandeur of duty, the power of character." And he again insists upon the paradox he had articulated earlier—in essays such as "Compensation," "Spiritual Laws," and "Circles" and a poem such as "Merlin"—that "though we know not how, necessity does comport with liberty" (*W,* VI, 4).

Having reiterated this belief, Emerson proceeds to explore the real "terror of life" which great men and nations confront (*W,* VI, 5). "Nature is no sentimentalist. . . . The way of Providence is a little rude. . . . [and] has a wild, rough, incalculable road to its end, and it is of no use to try to whitewash its huge, mixed instrumentalities" (*W,* VI, 6–8). He proceeds to offer a series of illustrations which demonstrate, for instance, the physical and genetic laws and limitations to which we are subject and concludes that "People are born with the moral or with the material bias" (*W,* VI, 12). As with people, so with groups and nations. English conservatives "have been effeminated by position or nature, born halt and blind, through luxury of their parents, and can only, like invalids, act on the defensive." On the other hand, the "strong natures, backwoodsmen, New Hampshire giants, Napoleons . . . are inevitable patriots" until—following the same cycle of growth-flowering-collapse which everything does—they decline (*W,* VI, 13).

Emerson pursues his analysis by admitting the insufficiency of his earlier view that "positive power was all." First he concedes that "Circumstance is Nature. Nature is what you may do. There is much you may not." The "negative power, or circumstance, is half. . . . The book of Nature," in fact, "is the book of Fate" (*W,* VI, 14–15). And he offers evidence from the recently established discipline of statistics and by pointing to a "system of the world" which inevitably, naturally, brings on "Famine, typhus, frost, war, suicide and effete races" (*W,* VI, 19). Any attempt to challenge or alter this system will appear "ridiculously inadequate." We cannot omit these "odious facts," this

Fate, this limitation. "A man's power is hooped in by a necessity which, by many experiments, he touches on every side until he learns its arc" (*W,* VI, 19–20).

But not all is gloom, doom, and determinism. He turns from these painful realities to explore the bounds and limitations of Fate itself. "If Fate follows and limits Power, Power attends and antagonizes Fate" (*W,* VI, 22). Further, he insists, "a part of Fate is the freedom of man. Forever wells up the impulse of choosing and acting in the soul." The power, of course, is Man's ability to think. "Intellect annuls Fate. So far as a man thinks, he is free" (*W,* VI, 23). The resource is there if Man will use it; and to the degree that he does, he will turn Fate's harm to his own good. A balance can be struck. Thought can not only defend the individual against the forces of circumstance; it can also marshal his "noble creative forces. The revelation of Thought takes man out of servitude into freedom" (*W,* VI, 25). There is also an echo of the earlier Transcendental soaring and vigorous self-reliance in the promise that "A man speaking from insight affirms of himself what is true of the mind: seeing its immortality, he says, I am immortal; seeing its invincibility, he says, I am strong. It is not in us, but we are in it" (*W,* VI, 26). And Emerson sustains the optimism of the passage by describing the inspiration with which the intellectual can ignite those who hear him: "we are as men in a balloon, and do not think so much of the point we have left [our past], or the point we would make [our future], as of the liberty and glory of the way" (*W,* VI, 27). The metaphor of flight is as crucial to the passage as its insistence on the primacy of process—which should call to mind his conception of flux, growth, change, melioration.

The positive note of the essay continues. After announcing that the moral sentiment as well as thought frees humanity, and suggesting that limitation might be better viewed as "the meter of the growing man" (*W,* VI, 30), the measure of his progress, he offers a refined definition of Fate: "a name for facts not yet passed under the fire of thought; for causes which are unpenetrated" (*W,* VI, 31). He gives a series of illustrations of these unpenetrated causes and arrives at the paramount example of Man's turning to his advantage that which he formerly dreaded—steam. He pursues this evolutionary turning of negatives to positives to the point of approaching the conventional notion of compensation which he had denounced at the beginning of that essay: "If

Fate is ore and quarry, if evil is good in the making, if limitation is power that shall be, if calamities, oppositions, and weights are wings and means,—we are reconciled." The next paragraph develops his insistence on the operating principle of "melioration," evolution, ascent: "The direction of the whole and of the parts is toward benefit, and in proportion to the health. Behind every individual closes organization; before him opens liberty,—the Better, the Best" (*W,* VI, 35). Here in bold terms is the predicate for the cyclical interpretation of history which lies at the heart of *English Traits,* his later—some might prefer mature—understanding of progress which had developed after the announcements of his early middle age.

He pursues the reciprocity of creatures and, noting what modern readers would label "ecological balance," insists as he had in *Representative Men,* for example, upon the connections each individual has with the events of his period. In his analysis, "History is the action and reaction of . . . Nature and Thought." Drawing on the commonplace of "two boys pushing each other," he observes that "Everything is pusher or pushed; and matter and mind are in perpetual tilt and balance." But roles change: the controlled becomes controller, and vice-versa. Mind can render any solid fluid, "and the power to flux it is the measure of the mind" (*W,* VI, 43).

At this point a note of mystery, even mysticism, informs the essay. Commenting on the sensitivity and impressionableness of the great person in touch with his times, he notes that "His mind is righter than others because he yields to a current so feeble as can be felt only by a needle delicately poised" (*W,* VI, 44–45). He explores several illustrations of these correlations and concludes that "One key, one solution to the mysteries of human condition, one solution to the old knots of fate, freedom, and foreknowledge, exists; the propounding, namely, of the double consciousness." And again, there is balance, compensation: whatever in nature impedes, even "lames or paralyzes you draws in with it the divinity, in some form, to repay" (*W,* VI, 47–48).

The concluding paragraphs of the essay not only accept this Fate but insist that we "build altars to the Beautiful Necessity, which secures that all is made of one piece." This "Beautiful Necessity" is not to be ignored, explained away, feared, or shunned. It is the "Law [which] rules throughout existence; a Law which is not intelligent but intelligence . . . it disdains words and passes understanding; it dissolves persons; it vivifies nature; yet solicits the pure in heart to draw on all its omnipotence" (*W,* VI, 49).

The defiant and self-reliant man may be absent, but in place of his vigorous cadences there is a calmer but equally assured voice chanting the same ultimate optimism and faith that the less experienced Emerson had offered in the late 1830s and early 1840s. The exuberance of the transparent eye-ball passage of *Nature,* the celebration of spontaneous, intuitive insight—Reason—may have given way to the more deliberate observations of the Understanding as experience imposed its lessons which had to be learned, yet Emerson remains a member of the Party of Hope. Perhaps a major part of the distinction we should note here is his very reliance on tough-minded analysis—Understanding—in grappling with the problem. The insight he offers is not the fruit of Transcendental vision, but of long and serious reflection. The same sort of rational consideration informs *English Traits,* a volume which embodies Emerson's different emphases as well as his new style and approach.

Published in 1856, almost a decade after he had embarked on his second trip to Europe, *English Traits* is Emerson's most sustained—that is, longest—prose work on a single subject. While it is certainly not of the caliber or importance of many of the earlier prose writings, it is critical for our comprehending the development of his views in his and his century's sixth decade. *English Traits* presents a refined and sophisticated view of the nation from which Emerson's family had come. Perhaps the largest question we must confront concerns the place the book enjoys in the Emerson canon. Further, how does one explain this vigorous nationalist's pondering the parent culture to the degree, for the length of time, and in the depth that he did? In a word, is *English Traits* an oddity or is it a logical and consistent outgrowth of his earlier thought; and how does it fit in with the new emphases of the late middle period?

It has been judged that there is "no better book by an American about Victorian England" than *English Traits.* The same critic argues, however, that the tough-minded pragmatism Emerson displays in the work is so at odds with his earlier Idealism—for instance, in *Nature*— that "a cautious scholar of the thirty-first century would scarcely dare assign them to the same pen" did he not know Emerson to be the author of both.[4] But it seems that to argue that there is such a disparity between *English Traits* and the earlier, more celebratory and visionary

writings is to ignore traces in the later work of the earlier Transcendentalism, and at the same time to miss Emerson's ability in the
early period to make practical—even pragmatic—empirical judgments. For example, such a view ignores the hard analyses of period
politics and society in lecture series such as "The Times" and in essays
such as "Politics" and "Self-Reliance." The point is that there is more
continuity than reversal—and certainly not repudiation—in the development of Emerson's views than is sometimes accounted for.

In many passages Emerson records his ambivalence about the relative
merits and deficiencies of English and American cultures, but nowhere
does he state his judgment more succinctly and clearly than in a short
section near the end of *English Traits.* He tells of touring Stonehenge
and its environs with Carlyle, who has just been holding forth about
how much an American might learn were he to confront and acquire the
superior culture of the Englishman. Emerson reports that he told his
host he was "easily dazzled" and that he "saw everywhere in the country
proofs of sense and spirit, and success of every sort." But despite his
admiration for the people and the country, he knows that once he
returns home he will "lapse at once into the feeling, which the
geography of America inevitably inspires, that we [Americans] play the
game with immense advantage." America is in fact "the seat and centre
of the British race; and . . . no skill or activity can long compete with
the prodigious natural advantages of that country, in the hands of the
same race." The "old and exhausted" parent "must one day be contented, like other parents, to be strong only in her children." Predictably, "this was a proposition which no Englishman of whatever
condition," certainly not Carlyle, "can easily entertain" (*W,* V, 275–
76).

Emerson's statement here informs the tone as well as the strategy of
the entire book. There is simply no denying that many facets of English
life and history, as well as Englishmen themselves, attracted him. For
example, after describing in Chapter 1 his impressions of the English
celebrities he had met during his first tour of the island in the early
1830s—figures such as Landor, Coleridge, Wordsworth, and Carlyle
himself—and then in the second chapter offering the standard period
literary account of his Atlantic crossing, he begins in Chapter 3 a
description of the merits of Old England. The reader is even told that
"The American is only the continuation of the English genius into new

conditions, more or less propitious" (*W,* V, 36) and is reminded of the enormous influence English writing has on period American reading tastes. There are, of course, qualifications such as the drawback of industrial pollution, but generally Emerson is positive in his chapters on "Land" and "Race" where he comments, among other matters, on the strength of English stock. In Chapter 5, "Ability," he tempers his basically favorable description by turning attention to an essential factor of English behavior, practicality. He points out Englishmen's impatience with "genius, or of minds addicted to contemplation," their "supreme eye to facts" (*W,* V, 80) and their fixation with property; but he does not condemn these. Nor is he critical of their achievement of social solidarity and of their prizing individuality even to the point of eccentricity, a major concern of the sixth and seventh chapters, "Manners" and "Truth." In "Character," the eighth chapter, he states his preference for their more cheery and contented attitudes, in contrast to the "much more . . . melancholy" (*W,* V, 128) postures even of young Americans. And in Chapter 9, "Cockayne," he compliments the English for having "little superfluity of self-regard. . . . [which] sets every man on being and doing what he really is and can" (*W,* V, 148).

It is here, however, about halfway through the book, that Emerson's assessments take a decided turn toward the negative. In regard to British colonialism he argues that "The English sway of their colonies has no root of kindness" (*W,* V, 151). He continues in Chapter 10, "Wealth," to notice their unabashed pride in wealth and its display, their aversion to poverty, their thrift and prudence, and, again, their fix on property. And toward the end of the chapter he warns of the danger of materialism, cautioning that "a man must keep an eye on his servants, if he would not have them rule him" and offering as a pertinent example the case of the machine unmanning its user. Specifically, "What he gains in making cloth, he loses in general power." Apparent gains bring liabilities, so we must sacrifice "in learning to tame and guide the monster. But harder still it has proved to resist and rule the dragon Money, with his paper wings" (*W,* V, 166–68).

England has prospered, "But the question recurs, does she take the step beyond, namely to the wise use, in view of the supreme wealth of nations?" (*W,* V, 169). He notes the paucity of measures she has attempted to remedy the ills brought on by her commercial society; but these have failed or been insufficient. In short, "Her prosperity, the splendor which so much manhood and talent and perseverance has thrown upon vulgar aims, is the very argument of materialism" (*W,* V, 170).

Emerson next turns his attention to the aristocracy, the subject of Chapter 11, and while he is generally kind in recognizing that conservative establishment's worth and its contribution to English society—for instance, in manners and in the collection and protection of cultural artifacts—he rejects the institution and its members for the vices in which they have indulged. (What American freeman could do otherwise?) More important, he suggests that their time has passed; the new commercial classes, the "untitled nobility possess all the power without the inconveniences that belong to rank, and the rich Englishman goes over the world at the present day, drawing more than all the advantages which the strongest of his kings could command" (*W,* V, 198). Oxford, the focus of Chapter 12, "Universities," receives tender treatment on the whole yet does not escape Emerson's old stricture about the inhospitality of the academy to genius. More significant and pertinent, however, he notes the modern deterioration of the "gentlemen" and scores the "seminaries" of Oxford and Cambridge for being "finishing schools for the upper classes, and not for the poor," as well as for their dedication to exploding anything "useful" in their curricula (*W,* V, 208–209). In one of the most biting and sustained attacks in the book (that in Chapter 13, "Religion"), he levels similar charges at the Anglican Church, taking it to task for its aristocratic fixation with forms and its clergy's lack of social conscience, among other deficiencies.

The fiery rhetoric of his earlier prose may be absent from his critique of establishments in *English Traits,* but his commentary is nonetheless piercing. The tone is quieter, the voice is more detached, less impassioned, yet the message is similar to those of earlier attacks, and the analysis is more consistently rational.

Decline is evident in modern English institutions and in the people. He sees the same low state of affairs in literature, the subject of Chapter 14: "In the absence of the highest aims, of the pure love of knowledge and the surrender to nature, there is the suppression of the imagination, the priapism of the senses and the understanding." And so "poetry is degraded and made ornamental." The words of Pope and Scott are derided: "The poetry . . . is low and prosaic; only now and then, as in

Wordsworth, conscientious; or in Byron, passional" (*W,* V, 255–56). Finally, a similar mediocre facility is evident in the London *Times,* his focus in the fifteenth chapter. The men of talent who set opinion by writing for the paper are educated to their craft. If we might revive the language of the earlier Emerson, they and their counterparts in other English establishments are thinkers, not Men Thinking. Like modern men of letters, they are not poets, visionaries, self-reliant men seeking to transcend. They are pedestrian. And the future is not theirs. Whatever England had achieved in the past, whatever few lights glimmer in the present, the fact is that this nation has long since reached her apex and is on the decline.

What Emerson was employing in his analysis of England was a cyclical theory of history[5] which he derived from a variety of sources: Greek thought, pre- and neo-Platonic philosophy, Oriental thinking, and, more important, the conclusions of period science and historiography, including the writings of Coleridge, von Herder, Cousin, Carlyle, and Stallo.[6] As we have seen in our discussions of some of the earlier essays and the poetry, Emerson clearly began to shift his concern from describing the individual, the self-reliant Transcendental hero capable of forging his own world, to defining the inevitable, shaping influence on human life by forces over which Man has little or no control. And destiny, Fate, determinism, naturalism were facts of existence he came to appreciate more fully as the years passed. Findings of period science, such as the views expressed in Robert Chambers's treatise on evolution, *Vestiges of Creation* (1845), had brought Emerson to a full acceptance of biological determinism about a decade before he published *English Traits.* He adopted and adapted the thought of Chambers and others and used it to underpin a firm conception of the birth-flowering-decline of races, nations, and institutions.[7] Central to this idea of the cycle was the notion that a nation possesses its "greatest mental power" as it begins its "initial ascent"; but as soon as these energies are codified into institutions, as inevitably they must be, the vitality of the new forces begins to diminish, the powers begin to recede.[8] Of course, Emerson the American as well as his own nation were explained and served well by such views. Whereas England was on the decline, America was on the threshold or in the early stages of its flowering. While even the vulgarity and materialism of the new nation might be excused as necessary conditions in the springtime of a culture on the rise, England's materialism, the decay and rot of her institutions, are symbols of her cultural autumn. England is doomed. America possesses the promise of the future.[9]

What we have in *English Traits* is a better reasoned theory to support the vigorous nationalism of Emerson's early period than he gave us in "The American Scholar," for example. With one crucial qualification: neither the individual nor any organization could evade or even avert the determinism, the Beautiful Necessity inherent in the unfolding of the law of the universe. The point is that life and the universe are in flux. Progress is real but neither constant nor steady. As we have seen from the earliest Emerson, achievements, arrivals yield new horizons, plateaus; people and institutions change, grow, meliorate. Now in *English Traits* there is a wider, more historical view. Just as people and organizations flow through successive growths, flowerings, declines, and deaths—springs, summers, autumns, and winters—so one civilization or nation, in this case England, recedes as another, mid-nineteenth-century America, emerges. The intelligent man must indeed, in Whicher's phrase, acquiesce to this inevitability, this Fate. But there is the assurance of ultimate rebirth, progress, evolution—even if one or one's culture might not share in it.

In *The Conduct of Life* (1860) Emerson centered his attention on the American scene; it had been sixteen years since he had offered prose essays on the subject. In the background of the volume one senses the disappointments and ugliness of the 1850s. There is a certain weariness, even resignation, in many of these essays and in the very strategies Emerson adopted to manage the problems he saw. Here as in the other writings of the middle period, the independent person's willingness to challenge and confront has been supplanted by the more deliberative and analytic observer who explicates and quietly refutes—and even plays "devil's attorney" (*W*, VI, 201) at times—in order to expose some major trends in American culture of the antebellum decade.

"Power" and "Wealth," the second and third essays in the collection ("Fate" is the first piece), are best understood as observations drawn from his examination of and vigorous participation in American life of the 1850s, and as manifestations of the principles and currents he explored, for example, in "Napoleon" and *English Traits*. Unlike England which is on the decline in the cycle of its history, America—the stage on which "Power" and "Wealth" are set—is in the growth phase of its ameliorative process. There may be much which is unhappy, even repugnant, in the materialism Emerson records in these essays; however, seen in proper perspective as marks of one period of development, the excesses and distortions of the flowering nation may be not only tolerated but embraced. His own country's materialism is sharply distinguished from that of England where it signals decline and impending death.

At times it seems as if Emerson is presenting a brief in defense of the Napoleons of this world, these men of "sympathetic attractions" who "carry nations . . . and lead the activity of the human race" (*W*, VI, 53). Arguing that all these successful men are *"causationists"* (*W*, VI, 54; Emerson's italics), he even quotes Bonaparte. "Imbecility . . . in the vast majority of men" makes them ready "victims of gravity, custom and fear" which renders them mere "bystanders" as the powerful "class enter cordially into the game and whirl with the whirling world" (*W*, VI, 54–56). Those in whom power manifests itself are in fact "sharing of the nature of the world" (*W*, VI, 56). They are "creative," people of "force" who naturally "take the best places" (*W*, VI, 58) in society and assert their strength and position in much the same way as a boy in school does or as good, disease-resisting trees and animals do.

At this point Emerson introduces a strain of nationalism into his analysis by recognizing the "advantages" of "The rough-and-ready style which belongs to a people of sailors, foresters, farmers and mechanics" (*W*, VI, 62), the same breed Whitman was celebrating in the 1850s. Warning that adhering to "English standards" can only rob Americans of their "sovereignty" (*W*, VI, 62–63), he describes those who possess "this coarse energy—the 'bruisers,' who have run the gauntlet of caucus and tavern. . . . Fierce and unscrupulous . . . usually frank and direct and above falsehood"; they are better fit to succeed in the brawling and mercurial antebellum world than are "churchmen and men of refinement." Confronting the realities of his nation's volatile and often corrupt arena, Emerson observes that "Politics is a deleterious profession. . . . Men in power have no opinions, but may be had cheap for any opinion, for any purpose." In such circumstances as the times dictated Emerson prefers the "forcible"—the bruisers—over the "civil"—the men of refinement. It is the "Hoosiers and Suckers [who] are really better than the snivelling opposition. Their wrath is at least of

a bold and manly cast." As calculating as Napoleon, "they proceed from
step to step" against the New England governors and legislators who
can only express their "sham virtuous indignation" in resolutions.
Having been more than an observer of the politics of abolition and
extension of slavery for the last decade, Emerson wanted to win, even if
victory must be had by means he may not have approved in better
circumstances. But then more genteel groups, he notes, "Philanthropic
and religious bodies do not commonly make their executive officers out
of saints" (W, VI, 64–66), not if they wish to survive, much less to
flourish.

Leaders, men of power, "cannot live on nuts, herb-tea, and elegies"
nor be satisfied by reading novels, playing whist, or attending lectures
and the Boston Athenaeum: "They pine for adventure, and must go to
Pike's Peak; had rather die by the hatchet of a Pawnee than sit all day
and every day at a counting-room desk (W, VI, 68). Central to
Emerson's thought is the idea that a "Strong race or strong individual
rests at last on [the] natural forces" most evident in the "savage life, in
explorers, soldiers and buccaneers" (W, VI, 69–70), for example.
But—and this qualification is crucial—the force which breeds power
must be managed, controlled, as it is "in the civil and moral man."
Emerson does not argue for unbridled savage force, however deeply its
roots might be set in nature, but suggests that good resides "in that
moment of transition, when the swarthy juices still flow plentifully
from nature, but their astringency or acridity is got out by ethics and
humanity" (W, VI, 70–71). Further, the powerful person must concentrate the force, avoid distractions, and also drill, which enhances the
power by "use and routine" (W, VI, 77) in order to gain control in the
"management of human affairs" (W, VI, 75). Finally, if one hears a note
of determinism in this description of the powerful person's manipulation of people and events, it also echoes in his suggestion that "this force
or spirit [is] the means relied on by Nature for bringing the work of the
day about." In his role as determiner, this powerful person is an agent
carrying out an "exact law and arithmetic" (W, VI, 80). The very
precision and predictability of one's achieving success are dramatically
different from the sort of intuitive soaring—transcendence—he emphasized in the early period. His self-reliant man of the 1850s is less a
visionary, a seer, than a master of life's economy: "The world," which
has so thoroughly touched Emerson in this prewar decade, "is

mathematical. . . . Success has no more eccentricity than the gingham and muslin we weave in our mills" (*W*, VI, 81), the homely and appropriate subject of the anecdote with which he concludes the piece.

This pragmatic, empirical, tough-minded analysis is probably one aspect of Emerson's thinking which, he tells us, "Some of [his] friends have complained" about when they noted that he "discussed Fate, Power and Wealth on too low a platform; gave too much line to the evil spirit of the times." They fear—as he reports at the beginning of "Worship," the sixth piece in the collection—that he has made "the argument of atheism so strong that he could not answer it." Emerson responds that he does not fear playing devil's advocate because he has "no infirmity of faith; no belief that it is of much importance what [he] or any man may say. . . . We are of different opinions at different hours, but we always may be said to be at heart on the side of truth" (*W*, VI, 201). Another factor which might help in understanding what he is about in the more important pieces in *The Conduct of Life* is the grounding the collection has in hard experience. We have already seen that during the 1850s Emerson was less reluctant to participate in the fray, and we should not minimize the effect on him of the realities he discovered there. Many of the signs of these volatile times were unattractive, indeed repugnant. But he evidently concluded that they could not be ignored or ineffectually challenged with mere rhetoric; stronger, more potentially successful strategies must be developed in order to guide the proper development of the young culture which seemed to be at a turning point; the measures and the times themselves were to be seen as part of the meliorating process. Flux, growth—in a word, progress—were inevitable, and a better day would dawn for the young culture. Here Emerson clings as tenaciously as ever to his essential faith in the moral unfolding of life and the universe. Willing as always to entertain all views—thus his skepticism—and even to advocate for the sake of clear understanding what he does not entirely accept, much less approve, he works from his consistent and profound belief that no time or culture or person, including himself, has once and for all cornered the market on reality.

We hear a similar sort of worldly wisdom in "Wealth," a companion piece to "Power," which it follows. Reflective of the entrepreneurship which has pervaded American culture since the industrial revolution, the argument of "Wealth" is abidingly practical, the result of experience. Wealth, "applications of mind to nature," is less the reward of industry and frugality, two of the underpinnings of the Protestant Work Ethic, than the result of "timeliness, in being at the right spot" (*W,* VI, 86) at the right time. Whereas "philosophers have laid the greatness of man in making his wants few," Emerson, in the expansive and optimistic spirit of his period, insists that Man "is born to be rich," to enjoy "the best culture and the best company" (*W,* VI, 88–89). "Poverty demoralizes" (*W,* VI, 90), compromises its victim's potential to act with integrity. Wealth, the "assimilation of nature" (*W,* VI, 93) to the powerful, is a means to control. And the desire to be wealthy is legitimate despite the unreflecting denunciations of "The pulpit and the press"; were those engaged in our commercial society to follow such advice, these "moralists would rush to rekindle at all hazards this love of power in the people, lest civilization should be undone" (*W,* VI, 95–96).

There are, of course, right and wrong ways of administering possessions, and Emerson recognizes society's responsibility to encourage the sharing of benefits by as many members as possible. But here in the essay he shifts from attempting to define and describe wealth and from discussing its public implications and uses to considering its broader implications and how to acquire it. As with power—and wealth is to be seen as one instrument of power—"The game requires coolness, right reasoning, promptness and patience in the players." Success in this game of commercial acquisition is not a matter of chance but of arithmetic, planning, control. "Property is an intellectual production" (*W,* VI, 99); "Success consists in close appliance to the laws of the world, and since those laws are intellectual and moral, an intellectual and moral obedience." Coin is "representative. . . . a delicate meter of civil, social and moral changes. . . . the finest barometer of social storms, and announces revolutions" (*W,* VI, 101–102). Of itself a dollar is or has no value but represents value, ultimately "moral values" (*W,* VI, 103). Rogues in power diminish its economic and moral worth whereas just men maintain or even enhance it. An unabashed laissez-faire capitalist, Emerson next extends his concern to political economy and judges the problems attending America's playing the role of haven for Europe's huddled masses as being the necessary compensation she must pay for her earlier rising fortunes. And he concludes by offering as mechanistic a set of rules for managing resources as ever Benjamin

Franklin could have conceived, noting finally in the spirit of melioration that "The true thrift is always to spend on the higher plane; to
invest and invest, with keener avarice, that [the person] may spend in
spiritual creation and not in augmenting animal existence" (*W*, VI,
126).

To wrench "Power" and "Wealth" out of context, however, would
distort Emerson's thinking in this period. "Culture," the fourth essay
in the collection, opens on a familiar dialectical note: "Whilst all the
world is in pursuit of power, and of wealth as a means of power, culture
corrects the theory of success." Recognizing that power distorts any
personality, Emerson proposes that such "inflammations" are reduced
by introducing balancing powers. There is a certain Fate or determinism being played out by unmerciful Nature as she "sacrifices the
performer . . . makes a dropsy or a tympany of him" (*W*, VI, 131) in
order to effect her purpose. Her means is each person's colossal egotism,
his "high conceit of his weight in the system"; he achieves power by
becoming fixated on developing his particular talent and so loses his
"relation to the world." Caught up in his progressively "narrower
selfism" (*W*, VI, 132–33), each person is determined to become what
he must.

Emerson, of course, does not reject egotism, this inevitable fact of
existence, but insists that having mastered his "specialty," one must
have "style and determination. . . . must have a catholicity, a power to
see with a free and disengaged look" the limitations "his private
history" (*W*, VI, 134–35) has for the rest of Mankind. Aware of his
incompleteness, each person will seek conversation and connection
with others, or Culture: "the suggestion . . . that a man has a range of
affinities through which he can modulate the violence of any master-
tones that have a droning preponderance in his scale." Culture converts
the distortions of self into harmony, "redresses" a person's "balance,
puts him among his equals and superiors, revives the delicious sense of
sympathy and warns him of the dangers of solitude and repulsion." And
so the "man of genius"—who is not the detached Transcendentalist of
the early period—is saved by "geniality" from the perils dictated by the
"organic egotism" (*W*, VI, 136–39) with which nature has endowed
him.

He continues the emphasis on Man in his social relations in "Behavior" and "Worship," the "flowering and completion" (*W*, VI, 204)

of culture. Recognizing the times as transitional—only one stage in the young culture's growth toward maturity—he judges period religions as "childish and insignificant or unmanly and effeminating" (*W*, VI, 207), largely because of their divorce from morality. (He had leveled similar judgments in public almost a quarter-century earlier in his Address before the Divinity School.) Confronted with the materialism of modern life, organized religions grope among the absolutes they have inherited and remain unable to remedy the period's ills. Exhorting them to "Forget your books and traditions, and obey your moral perceptions at this hour" (*W*, VI, 214), he goes on to reject "luck" and "circumstances" and to assert "cause and effect," the "arithmetic" (*W*, VI, 220) of life—a crucial qualification which is evocative of his recently emphasized rationalism. Man is directly, solely, and intelligently responsible for his life; "the dice are loaded . . . [and] the police and sincerity of the universe are secured by God's delegating his divinity to every particle . . . there is no room for hypocrisy, no margin for choice" (*W*, VI, 221–22). Life's last lesson is "necessitated freedom," and the religion of the present and future "must be intellectual. . . . Let us not be pestered with assertions and half-truths, with emotion and snuffle" (*W*, VI, 240–41).

"Considerations by the Way" continues the theme, but his weariness and disappointment with the times are expressed repeatedly, most pointedly in his desire that life be "sacred" (*W*, VI, 247) rather than merely amusing, as his culture evidently preferred. Utterly lacking any faith in the "masses," the unwitting conspirators and victims of the times, he judges them "rude, lame, unmade, pernicious in their demands and influence." They "need not to be flattered but to be schooled" (*W*, VI, 249). So much for the collective wisdom expressed by the democratic process in the discouraging times. The masses are "wicked" because they are "unripe" (*W*, VI, 252). Brawling America exhibits "coarse selfishness, fraud and conspiracy; and most of the great results . . . are brought about by discreditable means" (*W*, VI, 256). Matters are indeed so desperate that Emerson can "only insist that the man meliorate" (*W*, VI, 259). Here we have another statement of what may be the immediate, practical reason for his shifting emphasis in the middle period. Self-reliance and faith in the individual's reasonable prospects have given way to an abiding sense of humanity's limitations, precisely as his celebration of the Now has receded, has been overtaken by a vision of future attainment. The present may be tarnished;

however, he rejects depression, the jaundiced view, and embraces "sanguine youth and its glittering dreams" (*W,* VI, 265).

In 1857, the year after *English Traits* was published, Emerson composed "Illusions," the concluding piece in *The Conduct of Life.* Despite its brevity it is at once a forceful and revealing statement of the philosophical skepticism he had been increasingly drawn to, and a sturdy, unfaltering reaffirmation of his belief in Man's future possibilities and of his optimism generally. Emerson did not slip into despair or even resignation because the fire of his earlier Transcendental period had been banked by experience. In the same brave and forthright manner which he had revealed as a younger man, stating the truth as he saw it and challenging orthodoxy wherever he found it, Emerson in the middle period continued to face facts and tried to understand them in order to live with them.

The opening paragraphs of "Illusions" point up the deception he experienced during a tour of Mammoth Cave in Kentucky; the illusion of stars at the top of the cavern serves as a springboard to yet another reiteration of one of his basic beliefs, the subjectivity of perception. All people in all their ages are "victims of illusion" and "Life is a succession of lessons which must be lived to be understood. All is riddle, and the key to a riddle is another riddle" (*W,* VI, 313). His emphasis on skepticism may be greater in "Illusions," but the substance of his message is not much different from the statements he had made beginning in the early 1840s. He is sophisticated and honest enough to admit his own susceptibility to being seduced by a "new page" which for a moment he thinks will make the world "all brave and right" (*W,* VI, 316–17) but which proves to be as evanescent as other experiences. Who does not wish for certitude? In the same spirit as his humorist who maintained that God's two attributes were "power and risibility" (*W,* VI, 314), he suggests that the most powerful and accomplished people "have a gentleness when off duty, a good-natured admission that there are illusions" (*W,* VI, 317). As Emerson had insisted from almost the beginning of his public career, the condition of the universe is "incessant flowing and ascension" and so "'t is no wonder if our estimates are loose and floating. We must work and affirm, but we have no guess of the value of what we say or do" (*W,* VI, 320). Indeed, "we cannot even see what or where our stars of destiny are." Life does "seem a succession of dreams" (*W,* VI, 321–22).

The crucial point is that here in "Illusions"—as in "Fate" and other works of the middle period—Emerson does not break under the pressure which results from his growing sense of determinism. Inevitably, he must come back to the individual, and when he does he neither relieves him of his responsibility nor denies him his possibilities, his power to contribute to the quality and direction of his existence. Whereas in "Fate," the lead essay in *The Conduct of Life,* Man's ability to think had been his key to salvation, here in the closing piece the means is integrity: "In this kingdom of illusions we grope eagerly for stays and foundations. There is none but a strict and faithful dealing at home and a severe barring out of all duplicity or illusion there. Whatever games are played with us, we must play no games with ourselves, but deal in our privacy with the last honesty and truth. . . . Speak as you think, be what you are" (*W,* VI, 322). Man need not be a mere victim. Exercising moral tenacity and displaying a fortitude which might even be cruel for what it uncovers, humanity can arrive at an understanding, a version of reality which, even though it might not ignite the dizzying prospect of ultimate possibilities, will nevertheless refine its sense of identity and affirm its dignity.

Emerson concludes the essay with an equally crucial insistence. "There is no chance and no anarchy in the universe. All is system and gradation. Every god is there sitting in his sphere" (*W,* VI, 325). The universe is moral and existence purposeful. This is a quite different conception from the random and illogical forces which forge and form human destiny in the writings of some modern naturalists, for example. From Emerson's point of view, the winds which blow the leaves in Dreiser's metaphor[10] are not random. Actually, it appears that Emerson's ideas here are derived in some measure from period scientific thought as well as from his reading in theology and philosophy. And, surprisingly enough, his insistence on the laws which govern the universe appears to be in keeping not only with eighteenth-century Deism but with the empiricism of modern science. One should also notice another important difference in the late Emerson: the means to insight. Spontaneous, intuitive Reason seems to have receded as tough-minded, objective analysis—earlier classified as the Understanding—has moved to the fore.

Understood in its full dimensions Emerson's skepticism is not despairing. He preserved the essence of his Transcendental optimism even after undergoing life's cruel lessons and the diminishment of youthful enthusiasm. Poised and suspended, as the threatening clouds of the Civil War built while another twenty years of frenetic American life were about to crash in turmoil, he knew that the storm would pass and the sun rise on yet another period of change.

The last two decades of Emerson's life, what we might designate as his late period, were at once eventful and increasingly quiet. As he approached his sixtieth year, Civil War broke out in the United States and, like most of his fellow citizens, he was swept up on the waves of concern and patriotism. Four years after the appearance of his second collection of poems, *May-Day and Other Pieces* (1866), he gathered what he called the "twelve chapters" on *Society and Solitude* (1870). Many of the pieces in the volume offer eminently practical considerations—applications of the wisdom experience had taught him—on subjects of interest to his audience: the relative merits and drawbacks of "Society and Solitude"; the advantages and necessity of "Eloquence"; the dangers, but principally the merits of "conjugal, parental and amicable relations" (*W,* VII, 129) discovered in "Domestic Life"; the benefits and responsibilities of "Farming," though he warns that we "must not try to paint [the farmer] in rose-color" (*W,* VII, 138); as well as pointed advice on the art of selecting and reading "Books" and promoting fruitful conversation in "Clubs." The forceful voice of the cultural critic had not been silenced, however. In "Art" he once again condemns "superficial wants" and "superficial institutions" (*W,* VII, 57), and in "Works and Days," after celebrating the benefits of technology enjoyed by modern civilized Man, he calls to question the "corrupt and brutal" Politics and "shameful defaulting" of trade (*W,* VII, 165). He appears to be no less the moral critic of the Reconstruction era than he had been of the period before the War; now he announces that he "hate[s] this shallow Americanism which hopes to get rich by credit, to get knowledge by raps on midnight tables, to learn the economy of the mind by phrenology, or skill without study, or mastery without apprenticeship" (*W,* VII, 290). In place of such cultism, materialism, and superficiality, he insists—in pieces such as "Civilization," "Art," "Eloquence," "Works and Days," and "Success"—that his countrymen seek higher motives and purposes. The Transcendentalist's vigor has not disappeared, though his focus or emphasis has changed.

Emerson's health had begun to decline seriously as he approached his seventieth year, and that difficulty was compounded by the serious fire which in 1872 destroyed a good portion of the house in Concord where he and his family had resided for almost forty years. Despite the cares and troubles of the last dozen or so years, there were, in addition to the third and final collection of his poetry in 1876, two other volumes: *Parnassus,* his gathering in 1874 of favorite poems by others, and the next year *Letters and Social Aims.* The difficulty of producing this last work was recounted by his longtime, close friend James Eliot Cabot. Having had the task of arranging the book virtually thrust upon him, Emerson never was able to work up the enthusiasm necessary to perform it. After the fire, and probably before, "his loss of memory and of mental grasp," according to Cabot, made it improbable that he would ever do the job. After Emerson and his daughter returned from abroad in 1873, she and Cabot assisted him in producing the volume. Actually it was a retrospective collection of writings drawn from virtually his entire career, and Cabot put it together.[11] The volume includes some important work: "Poetry and Imagination"; "Social Aims," which in addition to practical advice on manners and getting along in society includes a vigorous defense of American behavior; "Resources," a strong denunciation of pessimism and an equally strong celebration of American achievements and prospects, which recall a more visionary Emerson; and four essays composed earlier but never published, among them "The Comic" and "Progress of Culture."

The physical and mental decline of these last years did not diminish Emerson's moral strength and sturdy independence. Despite the mellowing, he never compromised his integrity. Never for a moment repudiating his truths—however undoctrinaire they may have been—he knew they, like the views of all honest men, had been born of the times, places, and circumstances of his experience.

Chapter Six
Conclusion: Ever-Returning Spring

Unlike the treatment they have accorded several of the major figures of the American Renaissance whose reputations have survived into the late twentieth century, critics have fairly constantly recognized Emerson's importance and centrality to his times. He may have been controversial, even vilified and repudiated by some, but he was not neglected by his period, nor did he suffer the obscurity and sense of failure and frustration Melville did in an age not quite prepared for his thought and art. From the publication of *Nature* in 1836 to his death in 1882, Emerson enjoyed significant stature as an artist and thinker, and as a critic of modern culture. He was and remains the principal spokesman for the Newness—Transcendentalism—which helped breathe life into American thought in the late Jacksonian period; modern scholars seeking the meaning and import of this key intellectual movement must turn to Emerson's writings.

It is increasingly difficult to see how many serious nineteenth-century intellectuals, particularly Americans, could have ignored Emerson's thought. Evidently, they did not. Indeed, modern scholarship continues to demonstrate how pervasive his influence was. For example, one fashionable way of schematizing nineteenth-century American literary history is to divide it into the Party of the Past and the Party of Hope—to use, as one critic does, Emerson's own terms.[1] In such constructs we have on the one side Hawthorne and Melville, who are joined by their common perception of tragedy, their pessimism and generally dark vision of Man and his possibilities. Opposing them, forming a second current in our cultural legacy, are Emerson and, of course, the prophetic Whitman, with their essential optimism and faith in Mankind and its future. Such generalizations, however, must be used with great care and caution in the light of work which reveals a

Melville, for instance, much more responsive to Emerson than has been thought possible.[2] Even the classic tension between Yankee and Yorker—New England Transcendentalism and the often presumed, more commonsensical posture favored by the literati of commercial New York—begins to diminish when we recognize that the connections between these literary and intellectual centers were at least as numerous and important as were the distinctions between them. The point is that most serious intellectuals and artists of Emerson's day had to come to terms with him. To use one of his own favorite figures, he was at the center of the culture's circle, one of the handful who formed its hub. This is one way in which he effected the greening of American life suggested in the first paragraph of this book.

Writing less than a decade after World War II, Frederick Ives Carpenter charted Emerson's stature and influence as having crested prior to the First World War and concluded that by the early 1950s "his world influence must be measured rather by depth and intensity than by breadth and popularity." He suggested that Emerson's then unfashionable optimism was the principal cause for the pessimistic early twentieth century's declining interest in Transcendentalism and its chief spokesman.[3]

In the past thirty years, however, our appreciation of Emerson's thought and writing has gone beyond the understandings of those who center on the optimism, and especially the mysticism, of his early, radical period. Since Whicher and Bishop's work we have enjoyed a larger view of Emerson's development and learned to appreciate a more comprehensive version of his approaches and meanings. The full dimensions of his observations, if not his sense of tragedy, have been restored.

But as Emerson insisted, each generation has the right to seek its own realities—to read the past according to its requirements. Modernists and post-Modernists, their ability to perceive shaded by the holocausts of two World Wars, were perhaps compelled to hold Emerson in less esteem than his contemporaries did. But the world has once again survived its troubles, and now that we have a more realistic intellectual portrait of the man, perhaps we might listen to Emerson. Leaving earlier readers and their emphases, let us turn to some suggestions regarding the lesson and value of Emerson for the modern generation.

The revitalizing, renewing—in a word, the greening—he is responsible for seems certain to continue for each generation of Men- and Women-Thinking. There is, of course, the technical and artistic brilliance of many of his works, both poetry and prose, which will endure. In addition, Hyatt Waggoner, one of the better and more enthusiastic critics of Emerson's writing, has argued for his enormous influence "as spokesman and as catalyst" on Whitman and later poets; Emerson is, in his judgment, "the central figure in American poetry."[4] But equally important as Emerson's place in literary history is the fact that he addressed himself to problems which appear to be persistently— though often unhappily—central to American culture or, probably more accurate, to modern life.

If America is in the vanguard of modern civilization, and it seems reasonable to judge that it has been for at least two centuries, then the anxieties, agonies, and assertions we hear in Emerson's writing will continue to be pertinent because the issues he raises are: for example, his concern with threats to the rights of the individual continues to be of crucial importance in a world which appears less and less hospitable and respectful of the single, separate citizen; or, to approach the question from another angle, his distress over the frighteningly enormous, and growing, power of institutions—corporate, governmental, political, economic, and educational, to name but a few—is certainly relevant in our postindustrial technocracy which is as impersonal as it is complex and difficult to control. Few writers have seen key problems such as these with greater clarity than Emerson; he is among the handful of thinkers who have been capable and courageous enough to reach to the heart of such matters and identify the principles—not always ideals—at work in our everyday lives. As one generation after another spawns those ill-informed or wrongly programmed people who defend social and institutional violations of personal liberty for a host of well-worn if unacceptable, even absurd, reasons—enhanced efficiency, the needs of society and government, increased productivity, and what they generally call progress, to list but a few—Emerson's naysaying and high idealism ring true. He penetrates the partial observations and specious arguments of those who would obfuscate principle for narrow, selfish interest, or a supposed greater good, and brings to his reader a renewed sensitivity to the dire threats and moral resonances in even the most

seemingly pedestrian and remote events. As our increasingly deper-
sonalized, materialistic, and apparently amoral modern age unfolds, it
seems that we are in need of his insight and criticism even more than his
contemporaries were. This is not to suggest that readers today must
necessarily find his chief value in the spiritual or theological implications of his Idealism. Of course, Matthew Arnold's assessment of almost
one hundred years ago continues to hold true for some readers: "he is [and
remains] the friend and aider of those who would live in the
spirit."[5] Others, however, might derive a renewal equally salutary by
listening, for instance, to Emerson's version of the elusive American
Dream, which, he insists, initially and ultimately centers on the
individual.

His vision is not merely for fair weather and patriotic occasions. As
we have seen, this arch-spokesman of Democracy, this believer in Man
and the modern enterprise, witnessed the same sort of disillusioning
and embittering times which all people might reasonably expect to
undergo. The selfishness and materialism, the disregard of moral and
ethical principles, and all the other ills which he confronted in his
expansive, seemingly boundless period may be even more threatening
in our world which accepts ends and admits limits. And if his trust in
melioration, his essential belief in process and progress cannot help us
toward a larger view in assessing our frequently dismal and discouraging times, then they might lead us toward a broader understanding
which suggests that the American experiment itself is but one stage in
the evolution, the cycle, of civilization.

These seem to me some of the principal values of Emerson's vision
which will nourish our own and subsequent generations as we look
toward, in the words of his disciple Whitman, "Ever-returning
spring."[6]

Notes and References

Citations for Emerson's writings are offered parenthetically in the text. The abbreviations refer to the following texts:

CW   *Collected Works* (only vols. I and II have been issued: *Nature, Addresses, and Lectures* and *Essays: First Series*)

EL   *Early Lectures of Ralph Waldo Emerson*

JMN *Journals and Miscellaneous Notebooks*

L   *Letters of Ralph Waldo Emerson*

W   *Complete Works of Ralph Waldo Emerson: Centenary Edition*

Chapter One

1. The biographical information in this chapter is principally from Ralph L. Rusk, *The Life of Ralph Waldo Emerson* (New York, 1949), *JMN,* and *L.*

2. Joel Porte, *Representative Man* (New York, 1979), pp. 56–63.

3. Sheldon W. Liebman, "Emerson's Transformation in the 1820's," *American Literature* 40 (1968):144–45; Liebman offers a challenge to Whicher's image of a brooding Emerson during the 1820s.

4. Mildred Silver, "Emerson and the Idea of Progress," *American Literature* 12 (1940):2; Donald Koster, *Transcendentalism in America* (Boston: Twayne, 1975), p. 15. For discussions of Emerson's response to Jacksonianism see George E. Carter, "Democrat in Heaven—Whig on Earth—The Politics of Ralph Waldo Emerson," *Historical New Hampshire* 27 (1972):129; Arthur I. Ladu, "Emerson: Whig or Democrat," *New England Quarterly* 13 (1940):428–30, 433; Raymer McQuiston, "The Relation of Ralph Waldo Emerson to Public Affairs," *Bulletin of the University of Kansas Humanistic Studies* 3 (1923):19; Ernest Marchand, "Emerson and the Frontier," *American Literature* 3 (1931):162–63; and Perry Miller, "Emersonian Genius and the American Democracy," *New England Quarterly* 26 (1953):27–44; rpt. in *Emerson: A Collection of Critical Essays,* ed. Milton R. Konvitz and Stephen E. Whicher (Englewood Cliffs, N. J., 1962), pp. 77–78.

5. Sherman Paul, *Emerson's Angle of Vision* (Cambridge, Mass., 1952), pp. 227–28; John Q. Anderson, "Emerson and 'Manifest Destiny,'" *Boston Public Library Quarterly* 7 (1955):24–31. Leo Marx, who argues that Emer-

129

son supported the emerging industrialism of the period, points out that in the final analysis he called on his fellow Americans to renounce commercialism or surpass it (*The Machine in the Garden* [New York: Oxford University Press, 1964], pp. 230–31); and Marchand, pp. 167–73, notes Emerson's ultimate disappointment with Frontier materialism which after 1850 he observed firsthand during his lecture tours.

6. Daniel Boorstin, *The Americans: The Democratic Experience* (New York: Random House, 1973), passim, offers a lively description of period America on the move.

7. Sydney E. Ahlstrom, *A Religious History of the American People* (New Haven: Yale University Press, 1972), pp. 400–401.

8. Ibid., pp. 393–94.

9. William R. Hutchinson, *The Transcendentalist Ministers* (New Haven: Yale University Press, 1959), pp. 1–2.

10. Alexander Kern, "The Rise of Transcendentalism, 1815–1860," in *Transitions in American Literary History,* ed. Harry Hayden Clark (Durham: Duke University Press, 1953), p. 247.

11. Ibid., pp. 250–53; and Paul, pp. 14–18.

12. Hutchinson, p. 30.

13. Porte, pp. 211–13.

14. McQuiston, p. 41.

15. Rusk, pp. 366–69.

16. Among the most useful discussions of Emerson's attitudes toward slavery are John J. McDonald, "Emerson and John Brown," *New England Quarterly* 44 (1971):377–96; McQuiston, pp. 37–49; Marjory M. Moody, "The Evolution of Emerson as an Abolitionist," *American Literature* 17 (1945): 3–21; and Leonard Neufeldt, "Emerson and the Civil War," *Journal of English and Germanic Philology* 71 (1972):502–13.

Chapter Two

1. Robert E. Spiller, Introd., *The Collected Works of Ralph Waldo Emerson: Nature, Addresses, and Lectures* (Cambridge, Mass., 1971), I, xvi.

2. Ibid., Headnote, I, 74.

3. Porte, pp. 96–104.

4. Mary Worden Edrich, "The Rhetoric of Apostasy," *Tennessee Studies in Language and Literature* 8 (1967):549–57; Edrich somewhat overstates her argument for the importance of rhetoric in the Address; see also Porte, pp. 118–20.

5. Porte, pp. 106, 139.

6. Stephen E. Whicher, *Freedom and Fate* (Philadelphia, 1953), pp. 74–76.

7. Samuel Osgood, "it certainly will be called remarkable," *The Western Messenger* 2 (January 1837):385–93; rpt. in *Emerson's "Nature,"* ed. Merton M. Sealts, Jr. and Alfred R. Ferguson (Carbondale and Edwardsville, Ill.,1979), p. 78.

8. Richard Monckton Milnes, "American Philosophy—Emerson's Works," *The Westminster Review* 33 (March 1840):345–72; rpt. in Sealts and Ferguson, p. 103.

9. Quentin Anderson, *The Imperial Self* (New York: Knopf, 1971), pp. viii, 10–11, 27, 58.

10. A. Robert Caponigri, "Brownson and Emerson: Nature and History," *New England Quarterly* 18 (1945):368–75.

11. Perry Miller, "From Edwards to Emerson," in *Errand into the Wilderness* (Cambridge: The Belknap Press of Harvard University Press, 1956); rpt. in *Theories of American Literature,* ed. Donald M. Kartiganer and Malcolm A. Griffith (New York: Macmillan, 1972), pp. 341–42.

12. Paul, pp. 22, 34.

13. Robert C. Pollock, "A Reappraisal of Emerson," *Thought* 32 (1957):89–93, 97–98.

14. The eye-ball passage is well-described by Patrick F. Quinn, "Emerson and Mysticism," *American Literature* 21 (1950):408–14, as a "nature ecstasy" rather than a genuine mystical experience; it illustrates rhetorical "overstatement" of the source, Plotinus, rather than spiritual autobiography. Sherman Paul, p. 86, another of the more sensitive of Emerson's critics, has suggested that although Emerson was not a "visionary" mystic seeking merger with the Ultimate, he did seek mystical union as an epistemological necessity; rather than desiring to escape the world, he wanted to make use of it, ultimately in order to nurture the correspondence, or connection, between the "Me" and the "Not Me." And Warner Berthoff, Introd., *Nature,* by Ralph Waldo Emerson (San Francisco: Chandler, 1968), pp. xxvi–xxvii, lix–lxiv, lxvii, a more recent interpreter—who rejects the autobiographical elements identified by Jonathan Bishop, *Emerson on the Soul* (Cambridge, Mass., 1964), pp. 10–15—argues that Emerson's "major note is personal, elevated, and dramatic." He sees the eye-ball passage as "The great case of [the] projective and dramatic element of [Emerson's] style." As an Idealist Emerson is less concerned "to demonstrate the physical reality of an actual experience than to project the idea, the concept, of a certain constitutional transformation and purification possible to the self, the human ego. It is to project the idea of a *virtuous* conversion." The figure, he admits, is clearly but appropriately a grossly physical expression of "the Reason . . . stimulated to more earnest vision [in which] outlines and surfaces become transparent" (*CW,* I, 30). But rather than being autobiography, the eye-ball and related sentences are *"projective* and *performative.* They

are their own subject . . . a prose version of Romanticism's notion of style or voice in poetry that does not merely describe familiar realities but originates new ones." Other interpretations of the passage include James M. Cox's suggestion that it is a metaphor, image, or action, a "declaration of a change from being to seeing" ("R. W. Emerson: The Circles of the Eye," in *Emerson: Prophecy, Metamorphosis, and Influence,* ed. David Levin [New York: Columbia University Press, 1975], p. 61); Perry Miller has considered the passage in the light of colonial intellectual and theological history, arguing that such enthusiasm would have constituted infidelity in the seventeenth century, as it certainly would have to Andrews Norton. Such mysticism and pantheism would have been considered subversive in both periods (Miller, "From Edwards to Emerson," pp. 325–42).

15. Margaret Fuller, "Emerson's Essays," in *Margaret Fuller: Essays on American Life and Letters,* ed. Joel Myerson (New Haven: College and University Press, 1978), p. 245.

16. F. O. Matthiessen, *American Renaissance* (New York: Oxford University Press, 1941), pp. 64–66; even Emerson's biographer echoes the charge (Rusk, pp. 278–79); among the small group of readers which has challenged this conventional wisdom is Lawrence Buell, *Literary Transcendentalism* (Ithaca, N. Y., 1973), p. 158.

17. Among the critics who have commented on his lack of organization, early authorities such as George Santayana ("Emerson," in his *Interpretations of Poetry and Religion* [New York: Scribner's, 1900]; rpt. in Konvitz and Whicher, p. 34) and E. G. Sutcliffe ("Emerson's Theories of Literary Expression," *University of Illinois Studies in Language and Literature* 8 [1923]: 95–96, 115, 119) seem to have understood that Emerson was conscious of the devices he employed. Sutcliffe was close to the mark when he pointed out that Emerson was unwilling "to group things in a certain order when he was not confident that it was, in the highest sense, the right one," that Emerson's principle was that "no transition is better than sham transition." Further, although the absence of transition lends a certain obscurity to the writing, it does promote the aphoristic effect Emerson sought. Having mastered, for example, Blair's principles for oral delivery, by 1835 Emerson had discarded them and sought fresher strategies (Sheldon W. Liebman, "The Development of Emerson's Theory of Rhetoric, 1821–1836," *American Literature* 41 [1969]:204–205; see also A. M. Baumgartner, "'The Lyceum Is My Pulpit': Homiletics in Emerson's Early Lectures," *American Literature* 34 [1963]: 478–86). Lawrence I. Buell, "Reading Emerson for the Structures: The Coherence of the Essays," *Quarterly Journal of Speech* 58 (1972):59, 69, has astutely and convincingly argued that Emerson "was far more in control than at first appears, and that the appearance of formlessness is to a large extent a

strategy . . . to render his thoughts more faithfully and forcefully than direct statement would permit." This was no doubt the result of "his temperamental preference to be suggestive, rather than definitive."

18. Richard Lee Francis, "The Architectonics of Emerson's *Nature*," *American Quarterly* 19 (1967):39–53; rpt. in Sealts and Ferguson, pp. 166–72.

19. The structure or organization of his essay posed problems for Emerson. Writing to his brother William on August 8, 1836—*Nature* was published a month later—he said, "The book of Nature still lies on the table. There is, as always, one crack in it not easy to be soldered or welded" (*L*, II, 32). The flaw probably involved the seventh chapter, "Idealism," which lies between those on "Discipline" and "Spirit" (Spiller, Headnote, p. 4), and serves as a "specific concrete bridge" between them and "completes the pattern of complementary chapters" (Francis, in Sealts and Ferguson, p. 169).

20. This frequently quoted phrase is from Oliver Wendell Holmes, "Ralph Waldo Emerson," *Works* (Boston: Houghton Mifflin, 1892), XI, 88.

21. Merton M. Sealts, Jr., "Emerson on the Scholar, 1833–1837," *PMLA* 85 (1970):185.

22. Henry Nash Smith, "Emerson's Problem of Vocation—A Note on 'The American Scholar,'" *New England Quarterly* 12 (1939):52–67; rpt. in Konvitz and Whicher, pp. 60–61; for a consideration of this crisis in American society generally, see Ann Douglas, *The Feminization of American Culture* (New York: Knopf, 1977).

23. Sealts, pp. 185–86, 193.

24. Smith, in Konvitz and Whicher, p. 68.

Chapter Three

1. Caponigri, pp. 372–74.

2. Nathaniel Hawthorne, "My Kinsman, Major Molineux," in *The Complete Works of Nathaniel Hawthorne* (Boston: Houghton, Mifflin, 1887), III, 641.

3. Herman Melville, *Moby-Dick,* ed. Harrison Hayford and Hershel Parker (New York: Norton, 1967), p. 406.

4. Quentin Anderson, pp. xi, 14–15, 34–35, 56–58, 89.

5. Matthiessen, p. 9.

6. Pollock, pp. 110–11.

7. Paul, pp. 1–4, 34–36, 50.

8. Henry David Thoreau, *Walden and Civil Disobedience,* ed. Owen Thomas (New York: Norton, 1966), p. 62.

9. Bishop, pp. 76–77.

10. Modern readers have been generally unable or disinclined to defend this aspect of Emerson's thinking. The argument of Roland F. Lee, "Emerson's 'Compensation' as Argument and as Art," *New England Quarterly* 37 (1964):292, 296, that the essay "trails off into bathos" after betraying its promise of "a new sense of ethical motivation" is hardly challenged by Whicher's argument, p. 34, that the "principle of compensation . . . that 'all things are moral'" was a truth without which Emerson could not live. It seems that for most readers Emerson's position is even harder to rescue than his views on the moral sentiment.

11. Newton Arvin, "The House of Pain: Emerson and the Tragic Sense," *The Hudson Review* 12 (1959):37–53; rpt. in Konvitz and Whicher, pp. 46–48, 50–55; see also Bishop, p. 71; Edrich, pp. 552–53; and Liebman, "Emerson's Transformation in the 1820's," p. 141.

12. Thoreau, p. 2.

13. Harry Hayden Clark, "Emerson and Science," *Philological Quarterly* 10 (1931):229; Whicher, p. 89.

14. Whicher, p. 97; and Bishop, pp. 34–35.

15. Jack Null, "Strategies of Imagery in 'Circles,'" *ESQ* 18 (1972):265–66; Albert H. Tricomi, "The Rhetoric of Aspiring Circularity in Emerson's 'Circles,'" *ESQ* 18 (1972):278. This entire issue is a symposium on rhetoric in *Essays: First Series*.

16. William H. Gilman, Foreword, *Selected Writings of Ralph Waldo Emerson* (New York: New American Library, 1965), pp. viii–xv.

17. Paul, pp. 117–18.

18. Useful discussions of Emerson's use of dialectics appear in Bishop, pp. 79–80; Charles Feidelson, Jr., *Symbolism and American Literature* (Chicago: University of Chicago Press, 1953), pp. 158–61; Fuller, p. 243; W. T. Harris, "The Dialectic Unity in Emerson's Prose," *Journal of Speculative Philosophy* 18 (1884):195–202; W. T. Harris, "Ralph Waldo Emerson," *Atlantic Monthly,* August 1882, p. 247; Whicher, p. 57; Barry Wood, "The Growth of the Soul: Coleridge's Dialectical Method and the Strategy of Emerson's *Nature,*" *PMLA* 91 (1976):385–97; and R. A. Yoder, "Emerson's Dialectic," *Criticism* 11 (1969):313–28.

19. Buell, *Literary Transcendentalism,* pp. 160–63; Paul, pp. 117–18.

20. Buell, *Literary Transcendentalism,* p. 162.

21. Rusk, p. 300.

22. Lawrence Buell, "Reading Emerson for the Structures," pp. 59–63; and his *Literary Transcendentalism,* p. 65; see also Lewis Leary, "The Maneuverings of a Transcendental Mind: Emerson's *Essays* of 1841," *Prospects: An Annual of American Cultural Studies* 3 (1977):499–520.

23. Buell, "Reading Emerson for the Structures," p. 68.

24. Buell, *Literary Transcendentalism,* pp. 16–18, 100, 103.

25. Whicher, p. 26.

26. Ibid., p. 103.

27. Ibid., pp. 114–25.

28. *Moby-Dick,* p. 567.

29. Alexis de Tocqueville, *Democracy in America* (New York: Knopf, 1945), I, 53–58, 254–70, passim.

30. Daniel Aaron, *Men of Good Hope* (New York: Oxford University Press, 1951), pp. 14–16; see also his letter to his brother William, composed in the heat of the presidential campaign of 1840 (*L,* II, 357).

31. For a useful discussion of Emerson's views on reform see John T. Flanagan, "Emerson and Communism," *New England Quarterly* 10 (1937):243–51, 260–61.

Chapter Four

1. Hyatt H. Waggoner, *Emerson as Poet* (Princeton, N.J., 1974), pp. 68–70. As Emerson was to ask some thirty years later in "Poetry and Imagination," "Is not poetry the little chamber in the brain where is generated the explosive force which, by gentle shocks, sets in action the intellectual world? Bring us the bards who shall sing all our old ideas out of our heads, and new ones in" (*W,* VIII, 64).

2. Rosalie L. Colie, *Paradoxica Epidemica: The Renaissance Tradition of Paradox* (Princeton: Princeton University Press, 1966). Waggoner draws on Colie and rightly insists on our comprehending this poetic tradition within which Emerson worked.

3. Waggoner, pp. 139–42.

4. Ibid., p. 141; R. A. Yoder, "Toward the 'Titmouse Dimension': The Development of Emerson's Poetic Style," *PMLA* 87 (1972):259; Yoder argues that Emerson's approximation of the bard's wild freedom might even be viewed as a manifestation of "the essential link between Emerson and Whitman."

5. James E. Miller, Jr., *A Critical Guide to Leaves of Grass* (Chicago: University of Chicago Press, 1957), pp. 6–35; rpt. "'Song of Myself' as Inverted Mystical Experience," in his *Whitman's "Song of Myself"—Origin, Growth, Meaning* (New York: Dodd, Mead, 1964), pp. 134–56.

6. Carl F. Strauch, "Emerson and the Doctrine of Sympathy," *Studies in Romanticism* 6 (1967):158.

7. "Days," which was composed in 1851 and printed with several other of his short poems in the first issue of the *Atlantic Monthly,* has been

interpreted as one of a large number of poems which "reveal a more human Emerson" by virtue of their having been derived from reflections stimulated by his rather intense correspondence from 1840 to 1845 with Margaret Fuller and people in her circle. Specifically, Strauch argues ("Hatred's Swift Repulsions: Emerson, Margaret Fuller, and Others," *Studies in Romanticism* 7 [1968]: 65–103) that "Days" is linked to his correspondence with Fuller herself and expresses his lament about the failure of his relationship with her. Hyatt Waggoner, pp. 172–78, also relies on external evidence to explicate the poem and suggests that it is less imaginative, evocative, and "meaningful" than the essay to which he connects it, "Works and Days." In this context he sees the poem as an ambiguous plaint about our acceptance of the uninspired, about our failure to even attempt to reach toward the heights of our morning wishes.

8. Waggoner, p. 160.

9. Carl F. Strauch, "The Year of Emerson's Poetic Maturity: 1834," *Philological Quarterly* 34 (1955):353.

10. Carl F. Strauch, "The Mind's Voice: Emerson's Poetic Styles," *Emerson Society Quarterly,* No. 60, pt. 2 (1970):57, and his "The Year of Emerson's Poetic Maturity," pp. 373–74.

11. Strauch, "The Year of Emerson's Poetic Maturity," p. 372.

12. Yoder, "Toward the 'Titmouse Dimension,'" pp. 257–58, and Strauch, "The Year of Emerson's Poetic Maturity," pp. 361–64.

13. Waggoner, pp. 153–55.

14. Strauch, "Emerson and the Doctrine of Sympathy," p. 168.

15. Douglas C. Stenerson, "Emerson and the Agrarian Tradition," *Journal of the History of Ideas* 14 (1953):101–102, 106–107, 111.

16. Tony Tanner, *The Reign of Wonder: Naivety and Reality in American Literature* (New York: Harper and Row, 1967), pp. 19–23, 31–32.

17. Michael H. Cowan, *City of the West: Emerson, America, and Urban Metaphor* (New Haven: Yale University Press, 1967), pp. 4–19, 183–93, 210, 217, 231–36; Paul, p. 82.

18. Marx, pp. 231–34.

19. Strauch, "The Mind's Voice," pp. 53–55.

20. Joseph Warren Beach, *The Concept of Nature in Nineteenth-Century English Poetry* (New York: Macmillan, 1936), p. 348.

21. Strauch, "Emerson and the Doctrine of Sympathy," pp. 161–63.

22. Carl Dennis, "Emerson's Poetry of Mind and Nature," *Emerson Society Quarterly,* No. 58, pt. 4 (1970):147–51; for a discussion of the idea of correspondence at the heart of this interpretation, see pp. 139–46.

23. Tanner, pp. 19–45.

24. Strauch, "Emerson and the Doctrine of Sympathy," pp. 164–65.

25. Waggoner, p. 166, suggests that in "Woodnotes" as in "May-Day" "there is too little 'common-sense,' too little that the understanding can grasp." But Strauch, "The Mind's Voice," pp. 47–48, may be closer to the truth of the matter in his discussion of riddling.

26. "Emerson and the Doctrine of Sympathy," p. 154; Waggoner, pp. 118–20.

27. Yoder, "Toward the 'Titmouse Dimension,'" p. 264, offers a useful summary of the rejection of the poet here.

28. For a useful discussion of "The Sphinx" which challenges other interpretations such as Rusk's, see Thomas R. Whitaker, "The Riddle of Emerson's 'Sphinx,'" *American Literature* 27 (1955): 183–88. Refer also to the discussion near the beginning of this chapter of Emerson's conception of the poet.

29. Thoreau, p. 35.

30. *Works,* IX, 461.

31. Strauch, "Emerson and the Doctrine of Sympathy," p. 172.

32. In his notes to his edition of the *Poems,* Edward Emerson describes the startling night in New York late in 1866 when his father first read the work to him; Edward comments on his recognition of Emerson's "serene acquiescence [about] his failing forces" (*W,* IX, 489–90).

33. Carl F. Strauch, "The Date of Emerson's *Terminus,"* *PMLA* 65 (1950): 360–66, dates the first draft of the poem as 1850–51, and suggests that its subject is not old age but slavery; he sees it as the polar opposite of "Days."

34. Harris, "Ralph Waldo Emerson," p. 243.

35. Harold Bloom, *The Ringers in the Tower* (Chicago: University of Chicago Press, 1971), pp. 301–302.

Chapter Five

1. Whicher, pp. 170–72.

2. Porte, pp. 211–13, passim.

3. "Hawthorne and His Mosses," *The Norton Anthology of American Literature,* ed. Ronald Gottesman et al. (New York: Norton, 1979), I, 2060.

4. Howard Mumford Jones, Introd., *English Traits,* by Ralph Waldo Emerson (Cambridge, Mass.: The Belknap Press of Harvard University Press, 1966), pp. ix, xvii.

5. Philip L. Nicoloff, *Emerson on Race and History: An Examination of* ENGLISH TRAITS (New York: Columbia University Press, 1961), pp. 47–49, passim.

6. Ibid., pp. 51–93.

7. Ibid., pp. 102–26.

8. Ibid., pp. 235–36.

9. Ibid., pp. 133–34, 186, 244, 250–51 for discussion of England's fate; and pp. 176, 236 for America's future.

10. Theodore Dreiser, *Sister Carrie* (Philadelphia: University of Pennsylvania Press, 1981), p. 73.

11. *Works,* VIII, ix–xiii.

Chapter Six

1. R. W. B. Lewis, *The American Adam* (Chicago: University of Chicago Press, 1955), pp. 7–8, passim. Lewis, however, generally avoids the pitfall described below.

2. Merton M. Sealts, Jr., "Melville and Emerson's Rainbow," *ESQ* 26 (1980):53–78.

3. Frederick Ives Carpenter, *Emerson Handbook* (New York: Hendricks, 1953), pp. 252–54.

4. Hyatt H. Waggoner, *American Poets* (New York: Dell, 1968), pp. xii, 92.

5. "Emerson," in *The Recognition of Ralph Waldo Emerson,* ed. Milton R. Konvitz (Ann Arbor, 1972), p. 72.

6. Whitman, "When Lilacs Last in the Dooryard Bloom'd," *Leaves of Grass,* eds. Sculley Bradley and Harold Blodgett (New York: Norton, 1973), p. 328.

Selected Bibliography

PRIMARY SOURCES

The Collected Works of Ralph Waldo Emerson. Edited by Joseph Slater et al. Cambridge: The Belknap Press of Harvard University Press, 1971–. The two volumes issued to date in what promises to be the standard edition are *Nature, Addresses, and Lectures* and *Essays: First Series.*

The Early Lectures of Ralph Waldo Emerson. Edited by Stephen Whicher, Robert E. Spiller, and Wallace Williams. 3 vols. Cambridge: The Belknap Press of Harvard University Press, 1959–72. Includes lectures from 1833 to 1842.

The Journals and Miscellaneous Notebooks of Ralph Waldo Emerson. Edited by William H. Gilman et al. Cambridge: The Belknap Press of Harvard University Press, 1960–. Authoritative and invaluable, fourteen volumes have been published to date.

The Letters of Ralph Waldo Emerson. Edited by Ralph L. Rusk. 6 vols. New York: Columbia University Press, 1939. The value and authority of these documents are complemented by the *JMN,* immediately above.

The Complete Works of Ralph Waldo Emerson: Centenary Edition. Edited by Edward Waldo Emerson. 12 vols. Boston: Houghton Mifflin, 1903–1904. This standard edition is being replaced by the *Collected Works,* etc., above.

SECONDARY SOURCES

This listing is very selective. I have included basic studies—books and monographs—and refer the reader to additional bibliographical sources in the first section below. Few of the items in the notes, above, are included here.

1. Bibliographies

American Literary Scholarship: An Annual. Edited by James Woodress et al. Durham: Duke University Press, 1963–. Each volume of this annual review of scholarship has a section on Emerson studies. A useful supplement to Stovall, below.

Cooke, George Willis. *A Bibliography of Ralph Waldo Emerson.* Boston: Houghton Mifflin, 1908. Includes a chronological list of Emerson's writings; bibliographies of Emerson; an alphabetical list of single titles; a chronological list of separate works and editions, works he edited, and those for which he wrote introductions; notices and criticisms of his works; and other useful bibliographical information.

Stovall, Floyd. "Ralph Waldo Emerson." In *Eight American Authors.* Edited by James Woodress. New York: Norton, 1971. The best handy guide to Emerson scholarship. Includes sections on bibliography, editions, biography, and criticism. Use *ALS,* above, as a supplement.

2. Biography and Criticism

Bishop, Jonathan. *Emerson on the Soul.* Cambridge: Harvard University Press, 1964. A volume packed with close analyses and extended discussions of Emerson's assumptions and thoughts on the soul, and the effects of his conceptions on his art and intellectual development, Bishop's remains a major work with which the student of Emerson must come to terms.

Buell, Lawrence. *Literary Transcendentalism: Style and Vision in the American Renaissance.* Ithaca, N. Y.: Cornell University Press, 1973. Buell's study is among the more important by modern scholars. Emerson is only one of the authors he considers in this wide-ranging analysis of aesthetic theory and practice among the Transcendentalists.

Carpenter, Frederick Ives. *Emerson Handbook.* New York: Hendrick's House, 1953. The *Handbook* is an enduring basic introduction which includes sections on biography, the theories and workings of his prose and poetry, and his ideas.

Kern, Alexander. "The Rise of Transcendentalism, 1815–1860." In *Transitions in American Literary History.* Edited by Harry Hayden Clark. Durham: Duke University Press, 1953, pp. 247–314. This long chapter continues to be among the handiest, clearest, and most easily comprehended overviews of the subject.

Konvitz, Milton R., ed. *The Recognition of Ralph Waldo Emerson: Selected Criticism since 1837.* Ann Arbor: University of Michigan Press, 1972. An invaluable selection of the writings of his critics, this volume offers the scholar a profile of Emerson's reputation.

Konvitz, Milton R., and Whicher, Stephen E., eds. *Emerson: A Collection of Critical Essays.* Englewood Cliffs, N. J.: Prentice-Hall, 1962. This is a useful selection of some of the best Emerson criticism to have appeared before 1962.

Miller, Perry. *The Transcendentalists: An Anthology.* Cambridge: Harvard University Press, 1950. A vital collection of Transcendentalists' writings; Miller continues to provide a necessary base for the student, as well as a useful reference tool for the seasoned scholar.

Paul, Sherman. *Emerson's Angle of Vision: Man and Nature in American Experience.* Cambridge: Harvard University Press, 1952. This is a fundamental, influential, and well-regarded consideration of an essential aspect of Emerson's philosophical stance, his attempt by means of his idea of correspondence to reconcile the dualism he perceived.

Porte, Joel. *Representative Man: Ralph Waldo Emerson in his Time.* New York: Oxford University Press, 1979. This is the best biographical-critical study to have appeared in recent years, a necessary supplement to Rusk and others listed in this section.

Rusk, Ralph L. *The Life of Ralph Waldo Emerson.* New York: Scribner's, 1949. The standard biography by the editor of Emerson's letters, Rusk's study is basic, although it must be supplemented by the wealth of information provided by more recent scholars, such as the *JMN* editors.

Sealts, Merton M., Jr. and Ferguson, Alfred R., eds. *Emerson's "Nature": Origin, Growth, Meaning.* Carbondale and Edwardsville: Southern Illinois University Press, 1979. This invaluable volume, which centers on Emerson's seminal essay, reprints the text and presents the documents tracing its genesis, as well as selected major criticism from early reviews through the 1970s.

Waggoner, Hyatt H. *Emerson as Poet.* Princeton, N.J.: Princeton University Press, 1974. Waggoner's treatment is the best by a modern critic. In addition to comprehensive, penetrating analyses of the poems, he provides valuable discussions of Emerson's theories of poetry and the poet's roles, as well as their sources.

Whicher, Stephen E. *Freedom and Fate: An Inner Life of Ralph Waldo Emerson.* Philadelphia: University of Pennsylvania Press, 1953. Controversial since its appearance almost thirty years ago, Whicher's study continues to be a pivotal account of Emerson's intellectual development, one which all serious students must consider.

Index